The
REFLECTION
of Grace

The
REFLECTION
of Grace

Jenna,
may compassion write your story and Kindness be your signature.

Love and Prayers,

RENEE ELLER

Renee Eller

XULON PRESS

Xulon Press
2301 Lucien Way #415
Maitland, FL 32751
407.339.4217
www.xulonpress.com

Printed in the United States of America.

ISBN-13: 978-1-54566-020-1

DEDICATION

THIS STORY WAS WRITTEN FOR MY CHILDREN: three grew under my heart and three grew in my heart.

Zack—The very first human to ever call me Mommy. Later known as our very own cancer survivor and called "The Miracle Man" by his team of brilliant doctors in Mayo Clinic at the tender age of twenty-one. He is a hardworking, kind, and humble soul who is often lost in a good book. We lovingly call him "The Thinker" in our family.

Jacob—Our baby son. God truly knew I must have needed this gentle soul in our family the day He allowed me to give birth to him. He is a very ambitious and hardworking young man. He is kind and tenderhearted, always protecting his loved ones. He is the protector of his mother's heart.

Sarah—Our baby daughter. She is a gift from God for our huge family of blessings. She is always so thoughtful, loving, and kind. She is a hard worker often known as the girl ready to step up and take care of others. Though forever her dad's little "Princess," she will always be known as my mini-me.

Erin—The eldest daughter in our huge family. She is a wonderful mother of her two children and very loving. She is also very hardworking and has a fantastic personality. She always seems to make me giggle when I need it most.

Kristin—The second eldest daughter among our six blessings. She too has always been hardworking and a wonderful mother to her only child. My sweet mother-in-law always called her my little shadow when she was a child, and this melted my heart. She is a loving and very strong woman.

Laurin—She is our kind and loving daughter who is also a wonderful hardworking mother to her four children. She has a passion for reading, and I pray she will find herself lost in the pages of this book as well.

And dedicated first, to;

Dave Eller, the love of my life. The only man I could ever truly cherish. Thank you for being the very best part of me. Thank you for keeping me strong and always believing in us. Thank you for being the very best Christian husband, father, and grandfather I could ever have dreamed of. I pray you will always remember that I am who I am because you have lived.

And second, to:

All my brothers and sisters in Christ who have prayed with me, prayed for me, and encouraged me along the way in this wonderful thing called life during my Christian walk. I truly believe in the power of prayer, and I must always give God the glory.

And Finally:

In loving memory of my precious grandmother, Dora Potter. I am forever grateful to have been her granddaughter and namesake. She taught me to love God first and to always remain humble and kind. I will forever cherish every single moment I was blessed to have with my grandmother. I know she still lives on in my heart and soul as I make my own way through life's journey.

ACKNOWLEDGMENTS

SPECIAL THANKS TO MY PARENTS, BILL AND DORA Mae Dalton, for raising me to never forget where I came from and to never take life for granted. I am sure I learned to be a very strong woman because of my mother. Also, my dad was instrumental in teaching me to love without boundaries. For these things, I am forever grateful.

To my big brother, Tom Dalton, for being such a strong and honest Christian man in my life. He has been my constant support and tower of strength since my very first memory as a child. I always knew I could turn to him for the answers in life. He has always been my family compass when I needed to find my way, and for this I am forever thankful.

I would also like to give a special thank you to my Auntie Wanda Angel for her unwavering love and support throughout my life. She and her entire family have truly been my earthly angels.

CONTENTS

Chapter One

THE WOMAN IN THE MIRROR

THE WOMAN STARED AT THE FACE IN THE MIRROR. She wasn't even sure who the lady looking back at her was. Her eyes looked so sad and exhausted. As she looked deep into the eyes of this unfamiliar woman in the mirror, she began to wonder if this could really be the same little girl who once giggled her way into winning the many hometown pageants from years gone by. Could this reflection be the carefree young lady in college who so looked forward to the day she would take on the world to make a difference? She searched for answers as she studied the woman in the mirror. She was sure she would recognize some connection to this lonely soul looking back at her, but she could not find it. It was as if the two women had never met.

Yet, there was something so inviting and curious in the curve of her smile. Something very sad in her eyes. She felt she must investigate further. Could these unfamiliar feelings have something to do with her childhood? Grace had been a happy child growing up in Kentucky. She came from hard-working parents of modest means. Her father was a construction foreman and her mother taught school. Grace was an only daughter between two brothers. She had always been close to her family. She loved them, and they loved her. Life was good in Kentucky, and as for most of us, her childhood was the foundation of her entire life. The woman leaned back in her vanity chair and introduced herself. She actually heard her own voice speak out loud.

"Hello, my name is Grace. Have we met? You look so familiar to me." As Grace waited for a response, she simply smiled. Grace knew the woman in the mirror had very little to say. After all, it had been many years since she had felt heard by anyone. As this thought crossed her mind, she corrected herself. Her husband always heard her, felt her soul, and, loved her beyond words, but life had taken its toll on Grace and her youth. Grace was never one to worry about such trivial matters as youth and vanity, but she was feeling exhausted and uneasy about this crazy thing called life. Grace had always depended on her faith to see her through the most difficult times.

Today felt different from anything she had ever felt before. She put her head down and asked God to hear her prayers. God had always been there for Grace in her life. He was her salvation and her hope. He was her eternal strength. Her faith always sustained her, and she was thankful. Grace reminded herself of the many very serious times in her life, times of pain and unspeakable anguish. God was always with her, and He never left her. Having gone through times of such despair, Grace could almost feel the guilt of her uncertain feelings now. How could she ever have gone through the difficult times in life when the fear and pain brought her crashing to her knees, only to find herself feeling lost and confused now? What could be so different in her life now?

Grace was a very positive woman. She always felt her cup was at least half full in any given situation. Her family and friends were often amazed by her attitude during the tough times. This always made Grace smile. If there was one thing she had learned in life, it was that being positive was a choice. To her, a positive and grateful attitude was like breathing. She didn't have to think about it. Her attitude was as much a part of Grace as her next breath. She would start each day with these words, "Remember to count your blessings today, Grace … *not* your problems."

As she put her beautiful new pedicure on the cold travertine floor in her master suite, she was reminded of all the beauty that surrounded her every day. She and her husband had worked hard to have a beautiful dream home and all that comes with this gorgeous lifestyle. Grace knew this provided her with such lovely surroundings and the many comforts of life, but she never took any of this for granted. She had already learned something valuable in life, and she was more than appreciative of this precious knowledge. This was something she had always known deep within her heart and soul. But it took the heartfelt words of her firstborn son to truly explain it: "*People are more important than things.*" These simple words with a profound message have become a permanent part of her heart and soul. Such kind words to live by.

Grace had been very blessed with a huge, wonderful family. But with a large family, she never knew what each new day would bring to her heart. She knew she had many good days full of joy and pure happiness. She also knew the meaning of pain in a huge, beautiful family. Whether it was life's joy or its pain, one thing was always constant. Grace loved and adored her entire family. As a Christian wife and mother, she knew she could face anything this world threw her way. She more than loved and cherished her husband. After all, she had loved him for a lifetime and would continue to do so until her last breath. She had been with him her entire adult life, and for this, she was more than thankful.

When it came to her children, Grace always wanted to be their safe place to fall in life, and they knew it. This was a busy job because Grace had been blessed with a blended family. She would lovingly tell anybody she had six precious children in this life. Three grew under her heart and three grew in her heart. When any of her children came to her in pain, she always found a way of allowing their words to find shelter in her heart. The heart of a mother must be the safest place in the world for refuge. It is both trusting and trustworthy. It has an understanding and compassion without limitations. A mother's heart does not judge or hold grudges. It is unconditional in the purest form. A mother's heart must be one of God's most beautiful creations. It is His promise of someone on this earth to take care of His little lambs. Grace absolutely loves the mug from her youngest child. Her baby daughter, Elizabeth, gave her this mug for Mother's Day one year. Grace smiles every single time she reads the pink letters wrapped around her favorite beverage holder: "GOD COULD NOT BE EVERYWHERE ... SO, HE CREATED MOTHERS." Now, of course, she knew God *was* everywhere, but Grace still loved her special mug from her loving daughter.

As she leaned forward in her vanity chair, Grace heard a noise in the next room. It was the chiming of her husband's beautiful grandfather clock. One, two, three: the clock chimed eight times. This told Grace it was 8 a.m., and her husband was at work by now. It was confirmed. She was home alone, left with her thoughts.

Normally on these days, she had her days filled with taking care of two of their precious grandchildren. But her little blessings had some special plans with their dad, giving Grace a chance to catch up in life. As she went about her morning chores, she thought about the many years spent this way. Her husband worked very hard to provide a wonderful life for Grace and their six children. Grace worked just as hard taking care of their home and raising their children. She didn't mind the daily routine of life. She more than felt fortunate. She had once worked outside the home, took care of her husband, her three beautiful stepchildren, and their home. While she didn't have her adorable stepdaughters full time, Grace and her husband were lucky to have them four days each week. This was extremely exhausting once she was pregnant with their first baby together. However, she continued to work after having their first son. She was so pleased to work long enough to help pay off her husband's dental school loans as part of her contribution in their life together. Though leaving her career wasn't easy for Grace, she soon realized her baby needed his mother much more than any of the things her extra income would provide for him. While her husband had so much stress with his job, he always looked forward to golf on his off time. Grace understood his need for this stress-free recreation, and she never seemed to mind. She felt his love of golf helped him to relax and recharge. Grace was smart enough to know this would only make him a better husband and father. She was right, and he more than appreciated her understanding this need he had in his life. She always had a way of making him want to come home to her. He looked forward to seeing her tender smile as she would greet him at the door upon his arrival. She was always so excited to see him. She often forgot they had been married her entire adult life. Being with him was the most natural part of her existence, and she thanked God for her husband every single day.

As Grace continued with her daily chores, her mind began to wonder about the beautiful life they had built together. She had so many precious memories to revisit in her mind: The birth of her three precious children. Her love for her three beautiful stepchildren. So many memories to tell her story in life. Her family had been like a woven tapestry of the most beautiful material, threads of love binding them together on this earth forever. Each piece of material told a story. Each strand of thread held the stories together, giving life to the history of its very existence. Each character had a role in his or her story. Together, they made a life worth remembering: nothing grand, but, everything wonderful and deserving their place in the hearts of all those who lived it. She was reminded that it is the little things in life parents will forever cherish. Grace knew it would never be her college degree, dream home, nice car, or any other material things, she would ask for during her last moments on earth. Instead, she would want her family by her side.

Chapter Two

THE LOST POEM

AS GRACE CONTINUED TO TIDY UP, SHE CAME across something she had written several years ago. She couldn't believe her eyes. She had not seen this in so long, but it felt like only yesterday. She walked into her living room with her poem from years gone by. Should she even consider allowing herself to revisit this memory from the past? She took a deep breath and started to read her lost poem.

Because Is Not an Answer
God gave us our son,
Our precious baby boy.
He came into this world
To fill our hearts with joy.

Through the years he asked endless questions,
He was sure he just had to know.
"Because" is not an answer.
My son, he told me so.

Mommy, why is the sky so blue?
Will you hold my hand?

Can you see all the colors in a rainbow?
May I go play in the sand?

Mommy, did God make the sun and the moon?
Does He hang the stars in the sky?
Does He make the trees and the flowers bloom?
Do you think He makes the birds fly?

Mommy, does God watch over me?
Does He watch me when I play?
Do you think God really knows my name?
Can He hear me when I pray?

Mommy, does God really make the rain?
Does He make it fall from the sky?
Do you think God can see me now?
Can He see me when I cry?

Mommy, will you please answer me?
Can't you see I really need to know?
"Because" is not an answer, Mom—
Do you think God makes the snow?

I stood there in his room in Mayo Clinic
Just staring at the windowpane.
When he softly asked the question,
Mom, don't you just love the rain?

As the tears fell from my cheeks,
I turned to hear my son.
Mom, how can I have cancer?
I am only twenty-one.

Mom, can you believe this?
With chemo, my summer is gone.
Looking down, he shook his head and whispered,
I just really wish I could go home.

All I could do was pray
As I stood there by his bed.
God, please don't take my son.
I beg you, God, please take me instead.

I kept praying to the Lord above.
Then with His help, I finally spoke.
Son, we may not have all the answers yet
But we will never give up hope.

Though he kept asking endless questions,
So much he just had to know,
Sometimes we have no answers.
My son, he told me so.

Thank God for answered prayers.

Here are just a few memories from a very thankful mom.

The memories of this time in her life brought tears to her eyes. Grace always felt life was about moments in time. She felt each of us would go through life collecting our moments. Our collection would tell our story. Some people would choose to share their story with the world. Others would choose to put their story somewhere safe, somewhat hidden from the world, possibly tucked away safely in our hearts or somewhere deep in the corners of our minds, resting in a place we could visit them throughout our journey here on earth.

Some moments are so ordinary we often miss them. Yet, other moments are so significant, we are changed forever. The moment a doctor tells a parent their twenty-one-year-old son has cancer is definitely a significant moment. Grace will never forget this life altering moment in her life, in her precious son's life, in their entire family's life.

Zachariah was only twenty-one and near the end of his third year in college. He was very intelligent and determined to make something of himself. He had a kind soul and a zest for life. He never liked having his picture taken, and this usually showed in every single photo. He was never one to want the spotlight on him. He would often take extreme measures to prevent this from happening. He loved playing jokes on others, and the odd expressions of his younger brother, Frankie, in family pictures was more than proof of this. Just like most mothers, Grace was always so excited to get her photos back from their local film drop-off. This was when her children were much younger, before the convenience of our cell phones. Now everyone is ready to capture a precious moment and have it last forever. Cell phones can also allow people to look at their photos and catch their sneaky children in the act and make them pose again. This wasn't the case for Grace back when her children were much younger. She was a mother in need of technology to speed up its latest developments. She would no more than get the envelope opened when, there it was! Something her Zachariah had told her sweet Frankie to do for the camera. "Dear God, please help me understand why my sweet Zachariah insists on doing this to his brother in every single photo. Please help me understand why he has so much energy and refuses to keep his hands and feet to himself."

After talking to God about her high-energy son, Grace always smiled and thanked God for him. She secretly adored his personality and exhausting behavior. Grace knew he was never mean because he didn't have a mean bone in his body. She knew he just had more energy than he knew what to do with, which was fine with her. Then, one day in early spring, Grace noticed a difference in her son. She would stand by a window and watch her young son attempt to carry his backpack full of college books. Being a biology major meant he had several heavy books in his backpack weighing him down. He no longer had the bounce in his step she had always been so accustomed to. Her high-energy son had been replaced with an exhausted young man who was almost unrecognizable to his own mother. Grace tried not to over think this and assumed her concern was just coming from a worried mother. After all, Zachariah worked hard and studied so much. He was even earning his undergraduate degrees on multiple academic scholarships, while doing research for NASA. This must be normal. She had faith he would be himself again after he graduated.

Grace was planting her beautiful Mother's Day flowers by her pool when she heard a very soft voice behind her. It was Zachariah. He said, "Mom, I don't know what is wrong with me, and I don't mean to complain. But I am in so much pain." Grace looked up to see her son slumped over, holding his chest. His face was so swollen and red. It was obvious to her that he was having difficulty speaking, and his shallow breathing almost brought her to her knees. Grace knew something was seriously wrong with her son. She also knew she had to remain strong for him. Grace replied, "You aren't complaining, Zachariah. You are not well. I don't know what is wrong with you, but I promise we will find out. Let me talk to your dad and get you an appointment with a doctor."

She can still remember the look on his face. He had been going to doctors, and nobody seemed to know why he was continuing to get worse. In their defense, he had been an otherwise healthy young man. But the asthma inhalers and pain medication wasn't helping. Something much more serious seemed to be making her son ill. It was getting late, and Grace told her son to try to rest while she talked to his dad about his health issues. Grace would forever hear her own words from this very conversation. *I need you to hear me and not just think I am an overly worried mother. Something is wrong with our son, and if we don't get him some help, we are going to lose him. When I look at him, I can't help but feel he might have a blood flow problem. Do you have any idea who might be willing to see him tomorrow? I know in my heart that he can't wait for answers much longer.* Her husband listened, and after a very sleepless night, he got his son an appointment for 9 a.m. the following morning. Grace and her husband felt so relieved to get Zachariah in to see a local doctor known for his diagnostic skills.

After her husband had called home to give her the appointment information, Grace thanked God and then went to wake Zachariah. He wasn't in his childhood bedroom. Instead, she found her son attempting to rest upright in a recliner. There he was, surrounded by his many childhood memories. He was in the middle of the painted walls of their toy room overlooking a castle, an air hockey table, video games, movies and books, books, books, and more books. Grace had painted each wall with a different fun, colorful theme. It was obvious there had been so much love with each stroke of her paintbrush to provide a welcoming place her children could go and their friends could join in. This room held so much fun and laughter. If these coloring book walls could only talk, they would come to life with the hearts of so many children as they were growing up and finding their way in this wonderful thing called life.

But not on this morning. Not on this day. Grace heard no laughter. In fact, the silence was deafening. She could only hear the soft sounds of her son's shallow breathing. She could hear the pain in each breath he would take. Her heart was broken, and her fear of the unknown was screaming from within her soul as a mother. But she knew she must remain strong for her son as she approached him. She took a deep breath and just as she started to tell him he had an early morning appointment with an amazing doctor, she heard him speak first. "Mom, I don't even want to pretend like I know how much a person with cancer must suffer. But I only know if it's worse than this pain I am having in my chest and all the way through to my back, I won't be able to take it." As a mother, Grace knew her son was in trouble. She just had no idea exactly how much trouble he would have to face.

Chapter Three

THE DIAGNOSIS

THE DOCTOR KNEW ALMOST IMMEDIATELY WHAT was wrong with Zachariah. Of course, he had to do all the various tests, X-rays, ultrasounds, and blood work. He wouldn't share his concerns until he had them confirmed. Due to Zachariah's condition and the symptoms he had presented with, the doctor put a rush on the results. Zachariah was admitted to their local hospital on this very Monday afternoon. It was cancer—such an unkind and intrusive visitor with absolutely no boundaries. Both Grace and her husband were devastated and terrified over their son's health. Nothing in life can prepare a parent for this diagnosis concerning one of their children. Their world had come crashing down around them. As a mother, Grace knew it had always been her job to protect her children. She wouldn't allow them near the road when they were small. She made sure they all learned how to swim. She would always insist their friends would stay in her home so she would know their friends and what they were doing. She demanded good grades and curfews during the teen years. Cancer had never even been on her radar. Grace had been blindsided. She felt she had somehow failed her son. How could she have allowed this to happen to her own child? She was sure the mass in his chest should have been in her own and she prayed for this to happen. Grace would beg God to remove her son's tumor and allow her to take his place. As a Christian wife and mother, she knew this wasn't the way to pray. Still, her desperation took her mind to places she never knew she could go. She was sure if God took her son, she would need to go with him. After all, she was with him when he came into this world, and his first breath took her breath away. Grace could not let her son leave this world alone. She knew she didn't want to leave her husband and their other children, but she somehow felt they would always have each other and would take comfort knowing she and Zachariah were together in heaven until they would be together again. A frightened and desperate mother should not be held responsible for her thoughts of desperation during such unimaginable pain.

The moments turned into hours and then into days. They were blessed to have the best oncologist in their local area, and they were more than pleased to have him taking care of their son. But even he could not diagnose what type of cancer they were dealing with. His stress and concern over this unknown type of cancer was not lost on Grace or her husband. Unfortunately, Zachariah more than understood he had a very rare type of cancer, and this was not a good thing. Grace desperately wanted to take the worry from her son. After all, he had enough to deal with. Zachariah knew this about his mother and decided to make some things clear to everyone involved. Due to his age, he was the one who needed to legally make his own health decisions. He took this opportunity to explain his own plan of action. He told his oncologist, nurses, and other hospital staff he needed to be clear on a few things before he would sign anything. He knew he could include his parents on all the forms, allowing them to share his health information. This was the part he worried about. While he more than wanted his parents to know everything about the decisions he would be making, he needed to be sure nothing would be kept from him. As Zachariah started to speak, the entire room became his very own platform, with no interruptions. He asked if they knew his mother as he nodded in her direction. Grace wasn't expecting this because they more than knew the distraught mother in the room. Everyone agreed they had met his mother, so he continued. "I will allow both of my parents the legal right to know everything concerning my cancer as long as I always know first. Let me explain my reason. My mother would take this cancer from my chest and put it in her own if she could. But thank God she can't do this. She would also try to protect me from how serious this might become, and this won't help me. I have to know exactly what I am dealing with in order to fight this. She means well and she loves me, but this is my battle." Grace and her husband could not have been more proud of their son. He was mature and had faith beyond measure. For this, Grace was so very grateful.

By now, it was Thursday morning. After another sleepless night, Grace and her husband were facing yet another day, and still there were no answers on the type of cancer attacking their son. Zachariah had called his mother and ask her to come to the hospital even earlier because he needed to talk to her alone. Had it been up to Grace, she would never leave the hospital during the night. But his doctor and nurses felt he needed this time to process his thoughts and deal with everything he was facing. They were right. Zachariah would not allow his parents, siblings, or any of his loved ones see him emotional. He constantly wanted to protect them. Grace had no idea what to expect when she arrived at the hospital. To start with, her son had been moved to a different room! His nurses explained they had to relocate him to a huge private room. They said this was more than necessary to accommodate his many visitors. While he had his siblings, very close uncles, aunts, cousins, and grandparents by his side, his friends were just as amazing and wanted to be with him as well. This really made Zachariah smile, especially when the nurses said they had been asked several times if they had someone famous on the oncology floor.

After praying to God, Grace took a deep breath and entered her son's new hospital room. He looked so helpless to her. He had obviously not slept well through the night, and his breakfast was untouched. Still, he smiled when he saw his mom. He told her he really needed to talk to her. Grace asked him about his uneaten breakfast and explained to him the importance of keeping his strength up. He replied with a smile, "Funny you would say this, mom. This is one of the things I need to talk to you about while we are alone. This is now Thursday, and I happen to know you haven't eaten anything in days. I remember our lunch with dad on Monday when we were waiting for my results. You couldn't eat anything, and very little the day before." He explained to Grace he had a battle to fight. He said he couldn't fight this battle if he was worried about his mother's health, too. He pushed his breakfast tray back and said, "I will eat when my mother eats." Grace was stunned! Her son needed to eat and stay well-nourished for the fight of his life! How could he do this to her? The thoughts of eating something made her feel so ill. How could he possibly know what she needed, or even come close to understanding? He was her son. He was a part of her heart she could never live without. He had no idea she had to practically remind herself to breathe at this point. Still, he refused to eat his breakfast until she agreed to eat with him. He made it very clear she wasn't to go out in the hall and eat just enough to say she did. He said they would have breakfast together. And so they did.

After they finished their breakfast together, Zachariah said he needed to talk to his mom about a few more things before his visitors started to arrive. This was the beginning of a conversation Grace knew she would never forget. As he spoke, Grace listened to him. Making sure she would not miss a word, she prayed God would keep her strong for her son. "Mom, I couldn't sleep last night. I had so much on my mind. I need you to know something and hear this from me. Around 4 a.m., I had a talk with God. Mom, you already know I am a Christian, but this was a talk I had never had before. I guess I didn't feel the need until now. I need you to listen carefully now, Mom. I have made my peace with God, and I know I will be fine if it comes to this. I have already had an amazing childhood because of you and Dad. I'm not giving up, Mom. I am only making sure you know I am right with God if I can't win this battle. I can't leave this world if my mom is not going to be okay. I need your help with this, Mom."

Grace started to cry, and she could almost feel her son slipping away. Then, she heard him say, "This is the other part, Mom. I can't fight this if I am worried about my mom or any of the rest of my family. I know if this was my mom, dad, or any of my siblings, I would want to die. I need you to be strong, Mom. I need you to promise me you will stay strong and take care of my mother. This is the only way I can stay strong enough to do what I need to do." Grace wiped her tears away and made this promise to her son— and she kept it.

Thankfully, Grace had regained her composure just in time for her husband and the doctor to walk in. While they still could not diagnose his type of cancer, the doctor had some good news. After a great deal of time and persistence on his part, he had managed to get Zachariah into the Mayo Clinic. He said they would have their son flown by air ambulance the following morning. Word of this plan spread fast in their hometown, and his visitors would more than prove their love and concern for him. Grace and her husband gathered in their son's room, along with their five other children and some very close relatives and friends. They joined in prayer and shared some much-needed time together before he was to leave the next day.

Then, a nurse came to the door and explained they had a situation they had never had before. She said this patient had so many visitors waiting to see him, the hospital couldn't allow them in his room for safety reasons. She asked his visitors to please step out of his room because they had a plan. After a few minutes, the nurse came out of his room with a smile on her face. She was pushing Zachariah in a wheelchair and asked everybody to follow them. As the nurse pushed his new transportation down the long hall, Grace thought she heard some familiar voices. They stopped in front of a large waiting room and she noticed a sign posted on the glass door. The sign said, "VISITING ROOM FOR ZACHARIAH." She opened the door to a room full of people. They were practically on top of each other. The waiting room was filled with people in chairs, on laps, on tables, and all around on the floor. They had a difficult time leaving room to bring Zachariah in to see his friends. The young boy, who had always taken such extreme measures to keep the spotlight off himself, now found himself as a young man, the center of attention and loved by more people than they could even began to count.

The hospital said this had been the most visitors ever recorded for one patient in just one day. The nurse said they had given up on keeping a head count days ago. Grace saw

her son smile when this was discussed. He smiled. He actually smiled, and for a few moments during this difficult time,
Grace felt a comfort she had not felt in so long. She was
sure she would hold on to this image for a very long time.
Because he smiled, she could now breathe a little better. She
was finding her faith was becoming stronger again, and she
was so very grateful.

Friday morning could not come soon enough for Grace.
She and her husband were both packing frantically and
trying to get back to the hospital before the air ambulance
took their son to Mayo Clinic. Grace was so pleased that
her big brother and sister-in-law were taking their luggage
to Mayo for them. They actually took their two children out
of school so they could be there for Zachariah and the rest
of their family. Though they were fortunate enough and did
not need it, Grace was so grateful when her own parents
had even offered to sell their home and everything to help
with Zachariah's health care. The love for them was almost
overwhelming. Grace also truly appreciated her younger
brother for staying behind to see her son off when the air
ambulance arrived. This allowed Grace and her husband the
opportunity to get their own flights and travel arrangements
made to Mayo. Everything really was a team effort. It was a
holiday weekend, making travel plans more difficult. Grace
was praying they could get a flight. She couldn't imagine
her son arriving in Minnesota to be admitted to Mayo Clinic
without his parents there by his side. She remembered a
dear friend of theirs worked for the airline. Having lived just
next door to her sweet parents for so many years, Grace
hoped their daughter might be able to help them during this
most difficult time. Zachariah had actually grown up with the
daughter's son, and they were good friends throughout their
childhood. Their sweet friend worked tirelessly to get them

a flight, and words would never be enough to express their gratitude. Three flights later, they were very close to being reunited with their son.

As their third plane started to make its decline, Grace could feel her heart racing. She and her husband could not wait to see their son again. As the plane made its way closer to the ground, they could see something going on down below them. It was their son's air ambulance. Grace could see them transporting their son's hospital bed from the air ambulance to the ambulance on the ground. God had answered her prayers and brought him safely to Mayo Clinic. She knew it would be some time before she and her husband could actually get to him, but for now, just knowing he had landed would have to be enough. Both Grace and her husband knew this was a "God moment," and they praised Him.

Mayo Clinic was a wonderful place. The doctors, nurses, and entire staff made Zachariah feel very comfortable. It was a place of healing and hope. Grace knew they had made the right decision bringing their son to this place. After days of waiting for a diagnosis, the team of doctors finally came to his room with their findings. They were ready to share the diagnosis and their plan of action. As they stepped inside his room, Grace heard her son apologize and ask them if they would please give him a few more minutes. He explained to them he was on an overseas call with his longtime childhood friend, who was stationed in Kuwait. Zachariah felt he should take this call because his friend was serving our country and needed to know how Zachariah was doing. Despite the fact his team of doctors were shocked they had been asked to come back in a few minutes they respected him for putting his friend first. Grace knew the doctors more than adored her son after this happened. They had been given a firsthand glimpse of the young man they would all come to love and admire.

Mediastinal seminoma—Grace could hear the team of doctors explaining how rare this type of cancer was. She heard them explain it was so rare, they did not have enough patients to compare his case to, and they would not in his lifetime. She heard the word *lifetime*, and her son's entire life started to run through her mind. The doctors were still talking as the memories of her once high-energy child played on in her mind. It was like watching a movie in slow motion. She could feel the long labor and see his miraculous birth. She could see him bouncing through life with his high energy level. High energy. She remembered asking God about her wonderful son full of so much energy throughout his childhood. Now she understood. God was preparing her son for this battle in life. God knew he would need his energy and determination to face this. As the doctors continued to explain her son's condition, Grace continued to see his life through a series of scenes in a home movie. She saw him being baptized and loving Bible school. She could see her son as the drummer in his Christian band. She saw him graduating from high school with high honors and awarded multiple academic scholarships. She saw him running towards her to be held by his mother. She could see her precious son witnessing to his uncle during his own battle with cancer while living in their home. Zachariah was just a teenager and determined to share his faith with his terminally ill uncle. Just nine days before he passed away, Grace's sweet brother-in-law was saved.

Grace could still remember friends asking how she could allow this or manage this stressful situation in her home around her children. They were often worried about the emotional aspect. Grace would always answer, "How can I not?

He is my husband's only brother and my children's uncle."
Grace loved him as well. She always felt in her heart that
God was preparing her family in some way. She thought God
was teaching them how to love without boundaries because
they would be stronger for this. Besides, Grace knew it was
simply the right thing to do.

But looking back, Grace realized nothing could have prepared her for this with her son. She could never have imagined they were actually being prepared for this. As the team
of doctors continued to share their vast knowledge of her
son's condition, the scattered memories continued to play
on in her mind. Now he was in Mayo Clinic fighting for his
own life. Grace attempted to focus as the doctors said he
also suffered from a condition known as superior vena cava
syndrome, causing his blood clots. This was due to the large
size of his mass and the location of the tumor. Grace felt
numb, but she would not forget her promise to her son. She
would stay strong.

When Mayo Clinic said they would have to be aggressive
with Zachariah's treatment, they meant it. They explained
that they would have to hit him hard to save his life. They
made it clear that they couldn't worry about the long-term
complications of his treatment plan. They could only be concerned about now and his immediate health issues. Grace
stayed with her son during his first twenty-seven hours of
chemo. He had insisted she leave to rest, only to call and ask
her to come back to him. Grace could not get across the road
in the cold Minnesota night fast enough to be with her son.
She had only agreed to leave out of respect for his wishes.
She was more than glad he had asked her to come back to
him. She couldn't rest knowing her son was in the middle of
his first chemo treatment.

When she entered his room, the sight of her ill son took her breath away. He was very sick and needed her help getting to his bathroom. Grace rubbed her son's back as the poison running through his body made him violently ill. She continued to pray and keep her promise to her son. God would help Grace find an inner strength she never knew she had. They had shared twenty-seven hours of labor together to bring him into this world over twenty-one years ago. As a mother, she was more than determined to be by his side during his first twenty-seven hours of chemo. Grace knew she wasn't going anywhere until her precious son was well again.

Chapter Four

FAMILY SUPPORT

DURING HER SON'S STAY AT MAYO CLINIC, GRACE and her family faced many issues. Their younger son, Frankie, was graduating from high school. Grace and her husband couldn't leave their ill son in Mayo Clinic to attend his graduation. Nor did Frankie expect them to. He actually said he understood and would not want them to leave his brother. Grace was so proud of Frankie. Following in his big brother's footsteps, he too would be graduating with high honors, and he was being awarded multiple academic scholarships as well. Frankie had been through so much at a very tender age. He had lost some very dear friends. They were taken from this world way too young. This had broken Frankie's tender heart, and he was changed forever.

Grace always worried about Frankie, and the thought of missing his graduation broke her heart. She was so happy all four of his sisters would be there by his side. Their hometown knew about Frankie's big brother being in Mayo Clinic, so far away in Minnesota. Some very dear friends made it their mission to be there for Frankie. Grace was so pleased her sweet friend Jenny had even delivered some celebration food and snacks for his graduation party the night before the ceremony. Grace appreciated her taking the time to do this. Frankie had always been good friends with her only son, Brent, so it meant the world to Grace that Jenny was watching over Frankie during this time. Her very own hairdresser actually drove by to check on Frankie and his friends during his party. Grace was so pleased. After all, Susie was much more than their family hairdresser. She was a kind, loving soul, and Grace was so happy to call her a friend. So many good friends were kind enough to take more pictures than Grace ever could have. Her girlfriends Gayle, Dawn, and Shayla took so many beautiful photos. Grace felt they had captured almost every single moment, and Grace knew she would cherish them forever—both the photos and her dear friends. She knew her family had been blessed with the most amazing friends, and she was eternally grateful for their love and support.

Grace's dear friend Jenny called as her Frankie walked across the stage and told her she would be so proud of her wonderful son. His baby sister, Elizabeth, also called so her parents and Zachariah could hear Frankie's name being called. Because of this, they were still a part of this special day in their family, and Grace was beyond grateful. Grace turned speakerphone on, and she, her husband, and Zachariah listened to the graduation ceremony. She would never forget the moment when they heard Frankie's name being announced. As she looked at his dad and his big brother, she knew what they were thinking. The three of them were filled with mixed emotions. They were so proud of Frankie's accomplishments, and yet they were just as sad because they couldn't be there to celebrate with him. While they knew Frankie more than understood, they still longed to be there. Zachariah just put his head down and said he felt so bad for his brother. He said this wasn't fair to him, and he wished he could have been there for Frankie. Grace knew this was so typical of both of her sons. Despite Zachariah being in the middle of fighting cancer, he was concerned about his younger brother. Despite Frankie graduating from high school without his brother and his parents there to celebrate with him, he was worried about his big brother. Grace was just pleased to be part of this special day, even if it was by speakerphone.

Grace knew her very dear friend Jenny had called Frankie and Elizabeth to check on them before the graduation ceremony. Jenny said Frankie had thanked her when she called and offered to iron his graduation gown as she was ironing her own son's. She could just have her son Brent get it for her on his way home, and Frankie could either come and get it or she could deliver it to him. She was more than happy to help in any way she could, but he told her he would just "toss it" in the dryer. Grace remembered thinking that if this was the worst thing he had done while going through his graduation without her, she felt he would be okay. She later found out Frankie had worn his favorite green tennis shoes to walk across stage. She also knew his graduation gown was red. He later confessed that he had actually taken his nice black dress shoes to the ceremony. He knew these would be the shoes his mom would have him wear. Once there, he looked over at the black shoes in his truck and then looked down at the comfortable green shoes on his feet and smiled. He knew his mom would understand. Frankie also knew it was easier to ask for forgiveness than it was to ask for permission—well, at least concerning some things in life.

As his name was called, Frankie thought of his brother, Zachariah. He had a heavy heart knowing his brother couldn't be there. He couldn't believe his only brother was fighting cancer at the age of twenty-one. Despite his overwhelming sadness, Frankie knew he had a job to do. This was the one thing he could do to help his parents and the rest of his family during this nightmare. He took a deep breath. He held his head high and walked across the stage. His favorite green tennis shoes carried him every step of the way. When his brother found out about his choice of shoes, he smiled, just as Frankie knew he would.

Grace was so proud of all her children during this family crisis. Frankie and Elizabeth looked after each other while their parents were with Zachariah in Mayo Clinic. Elizabeth was only fifteen when everything happened. Frankie watched after her and drove her to and from school. While the rest of his friends were enjoying the end of their high school career and senior week, Frankie found himself the man of the house and responsible for his baby sister. Their three older sisters checked on them and made sure they knew they were always there for them if they needed them. Grace felt overwhelmed to have been blessed with such kind and loving children. They had many dear friends and wonderful neighbors checking on them as well, which brought a great deal of peace to Grace and her husband. Just knowing they had two lovely couples living next door on each side of them and another lovely couple across the road brought so much comfort to Grace. Their grandparents were also on the same lane. Grace knew their family had been given the best neighbors and friends they could have ever asked for.

Despite being worried about all their children and how difficult this had to be for them, Grace especially worried about Elizabeth. After all, she was the baby of a huge family. Elizabeth adored Zachariah, and Grace knew she must have been so frightened. Family and friends were often amazed to see just how strong Grace was during her son's cancer, but many people had no idea how much Elizabeth had helped her mother find strength she never knew she had. One day, when Grace least expected it, Elizabeth poured her heart out to her mother. Despite how much she was hurting, she kept control of her emotions and softly said to her mom, "You must know I have been really worried about Zachariah, but I think I am even more worried about my mom on some level. I am just as afraid of losing my mom as my brother." In this very moment, Grace realized she had not been fooling anybody. She especially had not fooled her baby daughter. She had thought her strong faith and her promise to her son had been enough to keep her strong, but her own fifteen-year-old daughter had seen straight through her. She knew she had to become even stronger and turn this over to God—to really trust in Him. She made Elizabeth a promise about this, and she kept it.

Grace was so appreciative of the support of so many wonderful people God had placed in her life. She knew she would forever be grateful for her lovely friend, Catherine. Catherine was a tiny lady with a huge heart. She was very outgoing and full of energy. Grace adored her bubbly personality and positive outlook. Catherine was a kind and loving soul with more compassion than she knew what to do with. Grace had always loved their talks and had often wished they could spend more time together. Their husbands were good friends and colleagues. This often brought the ladies together for dental meetings and out-of-town getaways. They always enjoyed every opportunity they had to visit. Grace was not surprised when Catherine showed up on her porch holding some delicious sweet bread. She had tears in her eyes. Catherine was heartbroken over Zachariah's cancer, and she was there to support Grace and the rest of her family. Catherine had always had a way of bringing such comfort to Grace, and on this day, she seemed to shine even brighter than ever before.

As Catherine expressed her love for Grace and her precious son as well as the rest of their family, she said something Grace would cherish forever. Catherine told Grace she was the kind of mother everybody wanted to be. Grace felt this was the kindest complement coming from her sweet friend because Catherine was an amazing mother of two wonderful children. Catherine was a teacher, and Grace knew how hard she worked because her own mother had taught school. Catherine had been very blessed to have an amazing support system; her parents lived nearby and were involved with her children. They worked so well as a family to meet the needs of everyone involved. Grace was always so impressed with the way Catherine seemed to manage so many different schedules simultaneously with such ease.

Grace adored both of Catherine's children and wasn't surprised when they both worked so hard in their chosen careers. As amazing and wonderful as Catherine was, she still had a special way of making others feel as though they were just as amazing and wonderful as she was. Grace just knew this came from her heart and soul. Grace took comfort and gained continued hope after their talk that day. A simple visit with sweet bread, a smile, and a heart full of prayerful compassion really can make a difference in this world. Grace was sure it had made a difference in her world when she put her head on her pillow that night and thanked God for her dear friend, Catherine.

Zachariah had made it through several months of very intense chemo. Grace would never forget the day he came to her holding his hair in his hands. Her son was actually fine with this. After all, he knew this was inevitable. But for a mother, it was yet another reminder of this cruel cancer that was attacking her son. For just a moment, Grace forgot her promise to her son. She didn't feel strong. She felt broken and tired of watching her son suffer. She felt the tears falling from her cheeks when her son wrapped his arms around her. He apologized for shocking her with his hair in his hands. He whispered in her ear, "I'm so sorry, Mom. I wasn't thinking when I showed you without any warning. Mom, I'm fine! I'm just thankful this isn't Elizabeth with her long, beautiful blonde hair." Grace realized he was still being strong for her. She knew this was so typical of her loving son. He really was thankful it was him and not his baby sister. Once again, Grace found her strength from her son. She thanked God for this and was ready to continue on this journey with him.

Zachariah not only had several months of chemo, but he also had to be on blood thinners the entire time. His doctors at Mayo Clinic needed to make sure he would not develop any more blood clots. Grace was so proud of him. He had such enormous faith. She often called her son her very own hero here on this earth. He remained in college during his battle with cancer and was an inspiration to all who knew him. Now, it was time for him to go back to Mayo Clinic for his surgery. His local oncologist, as well as his Mayo oncologist, felt this would be his best plan of action. They wanted to make sure he didn't have any cancer cells remaining in his chest once his chemo had ended. Grace knew God would take care of her son. Still, the thoughts of Zachariah being put to sleep to undergo thoracic surgery was almost more than her heart could take. She was still his mother, and he was her son.

Chapter Five

THE SURGERY

IT WAS AN EARLY OCTOBER MORNING WHEN THEY arrived at Mayo Clinic for Zachariah's surgery. Grace and her husband felt anxious and more than concerned for their son. Zachariah just wanted to sleep in the waiting room. He insisted he wasn't afraid and said he just wanted to get it over with. His biggest complaint was the early morning appointment. He was still drained from his chemo and exhausted from his trip to the clinic. Grace wasn't sure if her son was really this calm. She was just thankful he seemed to be ready to do whatever he had to do to get this nightmare behind him. As he slept in the fetal position with his hoodie pulled over his bald head, Grace prayed for her son.

Grace would never forget looking around the waiting room as her son was resting. Her husband had tears in his eyes as he saw the other families and the health issues their children were suffering from. While they had been through so much as a family over the last several months, they knew these families had been suffering for years. Some of these precious children had been fighting for their lives since their first breath. Grace knew to count her blessings and be thankful.

Grace realized her son might be right about remaining so calm. Maybe she should take a page from his book. He was so calm and relaxed as he waited in the wheelchair to be taken to the operating room. She would never forget the way he looked in his hospital gown with no hair from his months of chemo. He knew his mother was so worried. He took her hand with a gentle squeeze and said, "Please don't worry, Mom. I'm not worried. The doctor explained the surgery really well. He said it would take a few hours, and he would update you and dad throughout the surgery. He made sure we knew what to expect after I come out of the recovery room. He said I should expect to be sore, and I would just need to start moving as soon as I can tolerate it. According to him, the sooner I push myself to start moving after the surgery, the faster I will get to go home. Mom, I just want to get this over and get my life back. Everything will be fine." Once again, Grace listened to her son and promised to be there by his side when he opened his eyes.

Grace and her husband were told to wait in a designated area while Zachariah was in surgery. They were told they would be updated as the hospital staff was informed of their son's status. They waited and prayed. Hours and hours went by with no update. They spoke with a nurse who promised to get an update for them. Again, they prayed. After twenty minutes, she returned. She explained their son had just been taken to recovery at this time, and she would let them know when they could see him. Grace and her husband were so thankful to know he was finally out of surgery. They didn't understand why his surgery had taken so much longer than the doctors had predicted. They just knew he was out of surgery now and in the recovery room. This would have to be enough, and they just needed to be thankful and praise God. Again, they waited and prayed.

As the hours went by, they became very worried. Then, the surgeon came out. He apologized to them for taking so long and said he knew they had been very worried. He said he needed to explain something to them. He explained how he had no choice. Grace couldn't imagine where this explanation was going. She only knew she desperately needed to see her son. The surgeon explained his findings. He said he felt they had removed all of the mass that could possibly be left after the chemo. He said they would have to have this biopsied to make sure he had no evidence of cancer cells remaining. He said he also had to remove a portion of each lung to be safe. Grace finally felt relieved, until he spoke again. The surgeon said he had to take their son back to surgery and open him up again. He reminded them of the blood thinners Zachariah had been on for his blood clots. He said because of this, he had complications. They had a very difficult time attempting to stop his bleeding. He tried to prepare them so they'd have some idea what to expect when they would get to see their son. He made it very clear that he just wanted to get Zachariah through the night. After this, he would continue to get better.

Through the night ... this was stuck in Grace's mind. She couldn't understand. Her son was expecting to wake up from surgery feeling sore and anxious to start moving and getting his body stronger. Zachariah knew there was nothing to worry about. Grace was sure this must be a routine surgery for a place as well known as Mayo Clinic. *Through the night.* They must be mistaken. They must have her son confused with another precious son. As much as Grace wished there had been a terrible mistake, there wasn't. Zachariah was once again in recovery after a second surgery. The thoughts of her son having thoracic surgery took Grace's breath away. The thought of this being done to him twice in one day was almost more than Grace could take. The surgeon shook her husband's hand and excused himself. He needed to get back to their son. They were left to wait again, worry, and pray.

Grace knew she desperately needed her son to be on a prayer chain during his recovery. She called her friend, Jenny, for comfort. Jenny was a nurse, and Grace was sure she would have just the right words to comfort her. Jenny did comfort Grace and reassured her Zachariah was in such a great place with people who had the expertise to handle this situation. She promised to continue in prayer and let her know she looked forward to seeing them bring Zachariah home. Grace later found out this had been a long and sleepless night for both Jenny and her husband. While she had been so comforting to Grace, she and her husband were very worried for Zachariah.

As Grace and her husband continued to wait, the fear became almost unbearable. Her husband left the room to get her a cold drink, and she found herself alone with her thoughts. She began to pray again and ask God to wrap His healing arms around her son. As Grace continued in prayer, a nurse walked in the room and asked her if she was Zachariah's mother. Grace said yes and started to explain that her husband would be back in a few minutes. The nurse interrupted and said the doctor needed his mother to hurry. They wanted her to come to her son.

As Grace followed the nurse to the intensive care unit, she felt as though her legs would give out. Then, she remembered the promise she had made to her son and found her strength again. As she entered his room, she was shocked to see so many people working frantically to take care of her son. They were attempting to connect several different machines to him. She could see tubes everywhere on his body. Nothing could have prepared her for how swollen her son was. He was unrecognizable to his own mother. Grace was terrified she was going to lose her son. She started to step away for fear she was in their way and preventing them from doing their job. They quickly told her to get close to her son and start talking to him. She said she was worried she might upset Zachariah, despite his being in a medically induced coma. They told her it would be fine. They said he could still hear if she wanted to talk to him in his ear.

Grace knelt beside her son and started talking to him. She begged her son to fight for his life. She asked him to stay with her and not give up on his precious life. She told him she couldn't be on this earth without him. She reminded him how much his dad, his brother, his baby sister, and his three older sisters needed him. She reminded him of his grand-parents and all of his relatives and friends and their love for him. She reminded him of his dream to travel. She knew he had always wanted to backpack across Europe. Grace con-tinued to beg her son to stay with her. Then, she saw tears coming down his cheeks. Grace was upset and asked them why they said she wouldn't upset him! They said they had no idea exactly what she was saying in her son's ear, but they needed her to continue what she was doing! They said her voice and whatever she was sharing with him made her son start connecting. He was showing signs of determination and remarkable strength. *Strength*, Grace thought to herself. Yes, this is my strong and determined son. And she continued to make him hear his mother's prayers.

Grace would never forget the look on her husband's face when he entered the room. He was a dad, and his heart was hurting for his eldest son. He looked broken to her. He kept rubbing his son's smooth head. He whispered, "Just look what this cancer has put our son through. The chemo put his body through so much, and the blood clots have permanently harmed his health. He has fought so hard to beat this cancer. His surgery cannot take him from us." Zachariah's dad broke down and spoke through a flood of tears Grace had never seen before. Only she, as the mother of his precious son, could relate to it. He continued, "What have I done? What have I done? He had beaten his cancer from months of such intense chemo. We only agreed to this surgery to make absolutely sure he had no cancer cells left. What have I done? What have I done? What if the decision to put him through this surgery takes his life?" He then said something Grace knew he meant from his soul: "I just wish I was half the man my son is at only twenty-one." His dad never left his side. He continued to caress his arm, rub his bald head, and pray for his son.

Zachariah's dad was so worried that he made Grace leave during the night to rest some. He felt this was a must when Grace almost fainted in her son's hospital room. He thought she had gone to rest. But Grace was a *mother* and couldn't really leave her son. Still, she wanted to respect her husband's wishes. As Grace would discreetly look through the window to check on her son during the night, she realized his dad needed some time alone with their son. She later learned her husband was afraid their son would pass in the night, and he was sure Grace should not witness this. Thinking Grace had gone to rest during the night, her husband allowed her to relieve him during the very early hours of the next morning. It was still dark outside, but he knew morning was just over the horizon, and he understood Grace needed to be near their son again. He had no idea she had never really been gone.

Chapter Six

THE MIRACLE MAN

GRACE WAS STILL CLUTCHING HER SON'S ARM THE following morning when the sunshine started to send its new ray of hope through the hospital window. She put her head on the side of his bed and began to pray again. Then, she heard a soft mumbling sound. Her son had *survived the night* and was attempting to speak to his mother. This was very difficult due to his intubation. Still, she could understand his first word, "Mom." Grace could not get to her feet fast enough. As soon as she looked in her son's eyes, she knew he was frightened. After all, he had been told to expect waking up from his surgery feeling sore. Instead, he could only move his eyes. He couldn't speak clearly due to the intubation. He couldn't move because the surgeon had instructed his staff to restrain him to prevent injury. His doctor knew he would be frightened and confused if he woke up to find himself in this shape. Zachariah had two tubes in his chest to help with the drainage from his thoracic surgeries, and he continued bleeding. He had IVs in his arms and in his legs, as well. Because of his condition, they kept him completely flat in his bed. The doctor had instructed the staff to keep the bed elevated very high from the floor. He could only see the ceiling. Grace knew this, so she climbed on a step stool they had provided for her to allow her son to see his mother's face. She made sure she was smiling, despite the fact that she was crying for him on the inside. Grace actually made a point to keep her lipstick on so her son would assume things were at least somewhat normal and going to be okay when he first opened his eyes. She stayed strong for her son and kept her promise.

Zachariah attempted to speak again. "Mom." This was all he seemed to be able to mumble in his condition.

Grace answered, "I'm here, Zachariah. I'm here." He attempted to respond, but his words would not come out. She could see his desperation to speak, and she knew why. Her son needed answers. He tried to make a gesture with his hands, but with his hands and legs restrained, this too was more than frustrating for him. Grace finally realized he was asking for a pen and paper. She quickly provided this with the promise that he would be careful. His nurse said he would remove his right-hand strap as long as Zachariah understood he had to be extra careful and not try to move. He made him promise he understood he could only attempt to write on the paper to communicate with his mother. Zachariah closed his eyes several times to let them know he understood their instructions.

Grace held back tears as her son wrote, "What happened? Did it happen yet? Did they get all my cancer? Why am I like this? I love you, Mom. Is my dad okay?"

Grace took a deep breath and began to answer her son's questions. "*You are fine, Zachariah*. They did finish your surgery, and they just need to hear about the biopsy to make sure. The surgeon felt confident you are cancer free now. Your dad never left your side all night, and he will be back in a few minutes."

Zachariah wrote, "I need to know everything, Mom. They said I would just wake up sore after my surgery. What happened to me?"

Grace knew she had promised her son she would never keep anything from him concerning his health, and she had to keep this promise. As she struggled to read his almost indecipherable writing in his condition, she answered, "The surgeon said he had to also remove a small portion from each upper lung. Zachariah, you are going to be fine now, but they had to take you back to surgery to stop the bleeding. This was due to your blood thinners for your blood clots. They said this caused some complications after your surgery was completed."

Zachariah then wrote to ask if he could sit upright. Just as his nurse was explaining their orders to keep him in this position, his surgeon entered the room. Grace would never forget seeing the doctor grab his own chest and saying thank you as he was looking up after seeing her son. She later found out his surgeon was worried his twenty-one-year-old cancer patient might not make it through the night. She was also told he was a Sunday school teacher, which brought so much comfort to Grace. Grace thanked God for saving her son, and she continued to thank Him.

The look Zachariah gave his surgeon was priceless! Grace just knew he wanted to say, "You have some explaining to do." Zachariah immediately made it clear he needed to sit upright. His doctor knew he had a determined young man on his hands, and it was obvious he would need to start bargaining with this patient. "Zachariah, your body has been put through way more than we had originally anticipated. Because of this, I am going to need you to listen carefully and try to understand. The trauma to your chest cavity was extensive due to us having to operate twice within such a short period of time. It was an emergency surgery, and your body had no time to heal from the initial surgery."

Zachariah looked defeated, but only for a brief moment. Then he attempted to speak. He could not get his words out, so he motioned to his mom to hand him the pen and paper again. He wrote, "It's my understanding that the sooner I get these tubes out of my chest, the sooner I will get to go home. I need to sit upright to get stronger and get them out. Please let me do what I need to do."

The surgeon looked shocked and pleased at the same time. He responded, "I understand, Zachariah. But I need you to keep the tube we have down your throat just a little longer. If you will hang in there and cooperate, I promise I will remove it as soon as possible, and the rest of your tubes and IVs will follow."

Zachariah agreed to wait, but he told his surgeon he needed an approximate time he would be doing his extubation procedure. He was given his time frame, and he knew he could now focus on this plan. He could see the clock on the wall with his limited eye movement. He kept his eyes on the clock until the time was up. He immediately wrote another message letting his nurse know it was time to call his doctor because he needed his tube removed from his throat. The call was made, and his fight to get well began with Zachariah once again in charge.

After several hours, Zachariah was moved to his new room. The hospital staff explained to him that he must get up and walk as soon as possible. They said he had not only had thoracic surgery to remove any remaining evidence of any cancer cells, but he had a portion of each lung removed as well. Because of this, his lungs could collapse, and becoming mobile would be his only option to prevent this from happening. Two of the nurses were ready to take him for his first walk after leaving the intensive care unit. Zachariah made it clear he would rather go alone to regain his strength faster. Hospital policy would not allow this, but they agreed to compromise and have only one nurse walk with him.

The next day, she returned for his walk, but this time, he insisted on having absolutely no nurses helping him. Again, hospital policy would not allow this so soon, so again they compromised and allowed him to just use a walker to aid him on his second day. On the third day, his nurse came back to his room with a walker and asked him if he was ready for his walk. Zachariah smiled and said, "I don't need the walker today, but thank you. Now, I am going for a walk." As Grace watched her son walk down the hall with his hand gripping the handrail, she knew he was holding on to it with one hand while holding on to her heart with the other. It was on this day that Mayo Clinic named Zachariah "The Miracle Man," and his true healing began.

Finally, the day Zachariah and his family had looked forward to had come. His team of doctors said he could leave the clinic and go back home. They said he would need a chest X-ray and have his tumor markers checked every six months. They wanted him to look forward to his five-year cancer-free mark. His oncologist said he believed Zachariah and his parents would go back home and leave Mayo Clinic in their rearview mirror. As the rental car drove away towards the airport, Grace looked up just in time. She saw the sunlight reflecting off the mirror. As she continued to watch the sun's reflection, she saw Mayo Clinic in their rearview mirror. As the huge beautiful architectural buildings of Mayo Clinic slowly faded away, Grace noticed they were replaced with the smile on her son's face as he admired the gorgeous city. She simply smiled and thanked God as she felt the warmth from the sun shining down on her face through her window.

She knew they had taken this journey as a family together and because of this, they had been changed forever.

Zachariah had continued to show faith and strength throughout his ordeal, and Grace knew he wasn't finished here on this earth. Her son still had work to do, and there was at least one thing she was positive about. This world was a better place with him still in it.

Chapter Seven

COOKING WITH LOVE

GRACE WIPED AWAY HER TEARS AND PLACED HER long-lost poem on the living room coffee table. While she couldn't believe she had allowed herself to revisit this chapter of her life's journey, she knew it was somehow healing to do so. As a mother, she had lived so many years in fear of her son's cancer returning. He had been brave and embraced life.

Zachariah went on to graduate from college with a bachelor's degree in biology and a bachelor's degree in humanities as well. He packed his same old college backpack and went on an adventure of a lifetime. He first visited his brother Frankie, who was studying abroad in Spain. Next, he backpacked across Europe and saw things he had only read about in some of his favorite books. During his travels, he stayed in hostels and found his inner photographer.

Zachariah knew how fragile life could be. He understood the importance of living life and making memories. He later went on to graduate from Wake Forest as a medical laboratory scientist. He was awarded the university's most prestigious award, "THE BEST OF THE CLASS," and brought tears to his parent's eyes. As Zachariah made his way to the stage to give his acceptance speech, Grace thanked God not only for this outstanding award, but for bringing her son this far in life. There he was on stage thanking everyone for this award, and he once again found himself the center of attention. It was a place he never wanted to be, yet fate seemed to always bring him to this place. He thanked his parents for their love and support and made sure each and every classmate knew they too were deserving of this award. Zachariah never forgot his journey, and he always remembered to give God the glory. He continued his career as a chemist working behind the scenes to help patients who found themselves needing answers. He later married the love of his life and continues to make memories.

Grace could hear the clock chime five times. She knew her husband would be home soon, and it was time to start dinner. She loved to cook for her husband, children, and grandchildren. Cooking was a way to show her love for them. Grace was very nurturing by nature, and cooking gave her a chance to take care of her big, wonderful family. She would prepare each dish with such attention to detail. She knew all of the favorite recipes of each and every single one of her family members, and they loved this. She enjoyed making each one of them feel special in some way. Cooking and baking always gave Grace a target audience of her many blessings. Her homemade spaghetti sauce was always a crowd pleaser, and Grace loved to share her recipe. She loved to tease about the secret ingredient she would never give out to anyone.

Grace's Homemade Spaghetti Sauce

Two pounds of ground beef
Two chopped onions
Two cans of tomato sauce

Two cans of whole tomatoes
Two cans of diced tomatoes
Two cans of tomato paste
Two teaspoons of salt
Two teaspoons of sugar
Two teaspoons of parsley
Two bay leaves
One teaspoon of basil
One teaspoon of oregano
Half teaspoon of pepper
One cup of water
Cooked spaghetti
AND …
THE SECRET INGREDIENT

Grace felt she should always prepare food for her family with tender loving care. She always wanted each bite they took to remind them of her love for them. She prayed her cooking would always remind them of home. Grace always felt it was a good day when her home was full of their many loved ones, when joy and laughter filled each room and nobody could get a word in edgewise. Grace tended to laugh from her toes, which always made their grandchildren giggle. One of their grandsons actually said he found his grandparents in a huge children's pizza restaurant because he could follow the sounds of her laughter. This always made Grace smile. After all, if laughing too loud was her biggest problem in life, she was doing okay. Besides, her laughter was contagious, and this had to be a good thing.

As Grace continued working in her kitchen, she allowed her mind to drift. She always found it so interesting that the mind seemed to store precious memories of certain moments in time. She felt as though she had locked safes in her mind.

She knew she was the only person who held the key to open each safe and revisit the memory bank. She often felt as though she was the keeper of the treasures. As she moved about her kitchen, she remembered the many years she had prepared meals for her husband, her children, and their many friends. Grace loved the many adorable friends she watched grow up in her home. She could still see so many sweet faces and kind hearts in the corners of her mind. She wondered where the time had gone. She was sure she had only blinked. Now, some of these same children had children of their own. Some were still finding their way in life. Some had been taken from this world far too young. Grace knew one thing for sure: she would never forget them. They would forever have a special place in her heart and in her prayers. They would always have their very own special safe.

As Grace put the pasta on, she heard her phone ringing. It was her best friend, Gayle, and she sounded upset. "Can you believe this, Grace? This is so sad. It's just heartbreaking. I have no words. Are you still there, Grace? Do you need me to come to you?"

Grace could hear herself almost whisper, "No, I will be fine. I just need to hang up and I will talk to you soon." Grace was in shock. She was devastated to hear their dear friends had lost their precious son, Brent. Grace loved this young man, and he had been close with her children from early childhood. He had been very good friends with her son Frankie. He was the very first visitor to see Zachariah his first day in the hospital with his cancer. Grace would never forget this visit. Brent kept his sunglasses on, and she would forever remember seeing the tears falling from beneath them. Zachariah saw this as well. He was so pleased to have Brent there with him. He understood him and didn't dare ask him to take his sunglasses off.

Brent had such a tender heart, and Grace had always adored him. She had always felt close to him. She knew his tough guy act was just a front he used to hide his sweet soul from the world. He once told Grace that he felt Frankie was one of his closest friends. He said it didn't matter what his mood was or whether he said something he shouldn't, he could always count on Frankie to be the same understanding friend.

Grace would never forget the sweet smile on his face during this conversation. Everyone thought he was a very handsome and intelligent young man. He always had been and he had a way of pulling on her heartstrings. Grace was well aware Brent knew this, but she didn't mind. There was just always something about Brent. He could melt her heart before she could even see it coming. Grace couldn't believe this wonderful young man was gone so young. She knew she would forever cherish the years she and her family shared with him. Grace loved and adored his sweet family and would continue to hold them in her heart and prayers. After all, his mother Jenny had been a dear friend to Grace. The only comfort came from knowing heaven must have needed this sweet soul. He would be a guardian angel to all of those who had been blessed enough to know him. Now, Grace must help the rest of her family during this difficult time. She called her husband and explained to him what had happened. His staff immediately cancelled his patients, and he went home to be with Grace.

Chapter Eight

HE WAS MY FRIEND

GRACE AND HER ENTIRE FAMILY WERE HEART-broken. Her husband and their son, Zachariah, knew Frankie could not hear this from other people while he was alone on his job. Frankie had graduated from college with a bachelor's degree in cellular molecular biology and was now working in a lab. He had finally started to heal from so much loss at the young and tender age of eighteen. He would now be completely devastated and blindsided once again. Knowing how difficult this loss would be for him, they drove to tell him in person. Zachariah knew he would need to drive Frankie's truck home for his brother.

Words could never describe what Brent's passing did to Frankie. He was absolutely devastated. The loss of his dear friend was almost more than Frankie's tender heart could take. He was never the same after this. He was emotionally broken and afraid to care deeply for anyone again. When he came through the front door of their home, Grace wrapped her arms around her distraught son, and she could feel the weight of his body collapse in her arms. She could hear him say over and over, "He was my friend, Mom." Grace could feel his body tremble as she attempted to comfort her son.

Grace reminded him of just how much everybody loved Brent, and she knew in her heart Brent knew this. Frankie continued to cry out in such anguish for his dear friend. He knew the world had lost a great person. Grace knew heaven had gained a beautiful soul, and she prayed. She prayed for Brent's beautiful family in so much pain. She prayed for her own family in so much pain. She continued in prayer for all those touched by this loss. She knew if she and her family were having such a difficult time, the grief for Brent's own family had to be unimaginable. She knew a parent should never outlive one of their children. Grace realized she and her husband had come very close. Still, she knew they had only a glimpse into this pain compared to their dear friends. She prayed God would wrap his healing arms around them as she continued to watch over her sweet Frankie.

It was snowing the day they gathered to pay their respects. Grace remembered placing her rose and thanking God she had been so blessed to have Brent brought into their lives. She knew that because of him, they would never be the same. He had left his heart prints everywhere he had been, and Grace would be forever thankful. She knew she would always remember his sneaky grin, and she would never forget the sound of his laughter. In time, they would learn to speak of him and remember him the way they knew and loved him. They would share stories of his fun personality and would cherish every single memory. Grace knew her daughter Elizabeth was right when she said Brent wouldn't want us to stay sad forever. She said he would want us to remember all the things we so loved and adored about him. Elizabeth knew him well and had spent many young years with him, having been good friends with his only sweet sister. While Grace knew Elizabeth was right, she also knew Frankie was broken over his sweet friend, and he would never be the same again.

The doctors later said Frankie had known so much loss his entire young adult life. They said this started when he lost two dear friends so soon after turning eighteen years old in high school. Soon after this, his only brother was fighting for his life with cancer. Following this, his dad developed a very serious heart condition. His baby sister, Elizabeth, had gone through some very difficult times in her precious young life, so this had been a devastating time for Frankie. He loved Elizabeth and couldn't take it when she was going through such a sad time in her own life.

Despite their entire family and close friends knowing none of this was Elizabeth's fault or anything she had control of, as Frankie and Zachariah both would say, "Pain is pain." He continued to worry about her and feel overwhelming sadness. The doctor explained that the loss of Brent was almost more than Frankie's mind could take. Grace wasn't exactly sure what she could do to help her son. She only knew she was in a race against time to figure it out. His tender heart couldn't take much more. Grace prayed for her sweet Frankie without ceasing.

Grace would often think about something Frankie had said: "Pain is pain." Her son, Zachariah, had said this same thing during his own battle with cancer. They were both right about this. Grace felt one never knows what pain might drive someone to in life. She knew she had endured enough pain within her own family to know we all have our own journey in this life. We have so much to be thankful for as we make our way through this world. But Grace understood the happiness and joy in life must also share moments with pain and heartache. She had learned to allow her faith be her compass and guide her as she would navigate her way throughout the many moments during her life's journey. When life brought happiness and contentment, she thanked God. When life brought her sadness and pain, she looked to God for the answers and strength. Grace always knew her faith would sustain her. She knew as a Christian woman she would have glorious times where she would find herself high on the mountain, and she would also find herself down in the valley. Wherever she found herself, she knew God would be with her every step of the way.

Grace knew Frankie was down in the valley. As much as she just wanted to fix things for her son, she understood she could not do so on her own. She and Frankie would spend endless hours talking. She started to see evidence of her attempts in having an open line of communication. Grace was so pleased to see this. Knowing Frankie would come to her when he needed to talk brought Grace so much comfort and peace of mind. He opened up to his mother about so much pain. He talked about the fact that he had lost too many dear friends far too young. He admitted to her when he lost Brent, his mind and his heart just couldn't take anymore. Frankie said he felt ill every time his phone would ring. He said he was afraid of what he would find out about someone he cared for if he answered it.

Grace understood what Frankie meant by this. She too had become afraid of getting sad news. She knew her son's innocence had been taken, stolen like a thief in the night. He could no longer just be a carefree young man without a worry in the world. After the loss of his friends and his brother's battle with cancer, Frankie could not just assume he was invincible and nothing bad would ever happen. He told his mom he never wanted to forget his friends. He said they had been such an important part of him. He looked forward to the day he would think of Brent and remember the good times. For now, he still needed to find his way through the grief. As his mother, Grace was desperate to help her son work through the devastating pain. He was her first thought each morning when she opened her eyes and the last thought she had before putting her head on her pillow each night. She prayed without ceasing.

Chapter Nine

HEALING TAKES TIME

IT WAS 3 A.M. WHEN GRACE HEARD A KNOCK ON HER bedroom door. It was Frankie, and he needed to talk. "Mom, I know you have been so worried about me. I know you never rest these days. I just need you to know something." Grace could almost hear her own heart beating and then she heard him speak again. "Mom, I'm going to be okay now. I don't think I will ever really get over losing such a good friend. But I'm sure Brent would not want any of us to suffer any longer. I know he is in a better place, and I have to become more accepting about what has happened."

Grace was so thankful to hear Frankie say this. She was reminded of something she remembered hearing Brent's dad say. Despite being devastated over his son, he said he never felt closer to God than he did now because he knew God was taking care of his son until he would see him again. Grace knew she would not live long enough to forget this. Brent's dad had such a testimony of faith and his faith would see him through this.

Frankie hugged his mom and reassured his mother he was slowly healing. She made him promise he would come to her if he needed her and he did. After she closed her bedroom door she put her head on her pillow and thanked God for answered prayers. Grace slept on this night ... all night.

The next morning Grace awoke to another knock on her bedroom door. She felt a wave of panic come over her. Could this be Frankie? Had his break from pain been short lived? She jumped to her feet and opened the door only to find her precious three-year-old granddaughter, Emma, looking up with a smile on her sweet face. Emma said in her sleepy voice, "Are you ready for me Nana Gracie?" There she was with her favorite blanket and ready for her special day. Emma lived with Grace and her husband along with her big brother and her mommy. They were staying with Grace while Emma's mother was attempting to further her education. Melissa was the eldest child of this big family, and she had been blessed with two beautiful children. Grace didn't mind helping her stepdaughter during this time in her life. After all, this just meant she would have special bonding time with their grandchildren.

The grandchildren were only eight months old and four years old when they moved in with Grace and their Pops. Grace would wake up each morning to their sweet little faces. Both ready to take on the world and all it had to offer. Emma's big brother was less than four years older than her, but he loved to remind her of his seniority in life. Joshy was an amazing little boy. He was very active and seemed to be good in every sport he attempted. He was a cute little blonde with the most adorable little grin. He was always up to something and proud of it. Joshy was very smart, but they later found out he did not care too much for school. Grace thought he might have liked the social part, but he resented the homework. Every single school night was a battleground, and Joshy was ready to defend himself against the evil homework. But for now, he was in school, and it was time for Grace and Emma to start their day.

Having been so worried about her talk with Frankie only hours before, Emma was a beautiful distraction. Frankie had really enjoyed both Joshy and Emma. He had once told Grace they gave him hope when he was going through so much pain. They were proof that life goes on as we find our new normal when emerging from a place of such grief. Grace knew her precious grandchildren had saved her as well. The loss of Brent still took her breath away. One sweet hug from Joshy or Emma helped her breathe again. She knew they had been brought to her home at just the right time. While to most people, it seemed as though Grace and her husband were helping Melissa and her two babies, Grace knew they were really helping her. Children just have a way of lessening the pain in life. Grace was more than thankful for her little blessings in disguise. She thanked God for them every single day.

As Grace scooped her little Emma up in her arms, she said, "What are we going to do today, Sweet Baby Girl Angel Kisses?"

Miss Emma answered with such conviction, "I think we need to polish my fingernails and toenails and make some chocolate chip cookies. Later, we can go get Bubby from school, and then we can go get a kid's meal." Grace smiled as she agreed with this fabulous plan. As they walked to the kitchen to get started, Grace asked Emma her four daily questions:

Grace: Who made you so beautiful?
Emma: God did.
Grace: Who made you so smart?
Emma: God did.
Grace: Who made you so kind?
Emma: God did.
Grace: Now, what do we say?
Emma: Thank You, God, for everything … and Emma!

Emma loved this part of their day. As a grandmother, Grace loved this beautiful tradition they had shared together. Grace felt it was important to share her faith with her family. Besides, if God had blessed her with this precious little grand-daughter and had trusted Grace to take care of her, she knew the least she could do was to teach Emma about Him.

As Emma helped Grace in the kitchen, she talked about her Pops, aunts, uncles, and cousins. Emma loved having a big family, and she especially loved their time together. Grace always looked forward to family dinners or grilling by the pool. Her stepdaughter, Leigh, was next to the oldest. She had one beautiful daughter, Brianna. She was a lovely, mature young lady, and Grace really enjoyed her visits. Grace adored both Leigh and Brianna.

Grace's youngest stepdaughter, Brooke, had four children. She had been blessed with a son, Brad, a daughter, Paige, a son, Jay, and a baby daughter, McKenna. Brad was now a young man with a busy life of his own. While Grace and her husband missed spending time with him, they understood. Besides, with their huge family, they had lots of love to share and blessings to keep them busy. Paige was a beautiful teenager with personality and then some. She could always light up a room and make Grace smile. Sweet Jay had such a tender heart. The thought of someone having hurt feelings would take his breath away. He loved art and would work on his many projects for hours. He loved to surprise Grace and the rest of his family with his masterpieces. Grace was always so proud of him, and he knew it. As for sweet McKenna, she simply knew how to melt the hearts of all who loved her. She was a beautiful little girl with gorgeous dark curls and the cutest personality. Grace knew it was a great day when she had all of her loved ones in the same place. This wasn't always an easy task, but it was worth accomplishing. She looked forward to having even more beautiful little ones from her younger children. After all, life was about family, and Grace cherished hers.

"Yikes! I'm sorry, Nana Gracie." Grace turned to find Emma trying to clean the egg-covered floor.

Grace saw the tears in Emma's little eyes, and she knew she needed to rescue her sweet granddaughter. "It's okay, Emma. Did you drop the eggs on purpose?"

Emma looked so shocked as she said, "No I would never do this on purpose!"

Grace then explained, "All of us make mistakes some-times, sweetie. Even adults make mistakes, Emma. We should work together to clean this mess up."

Emma smiled and said this was a great idea. As they started cleaning together, Grace just so happened made sure she dropped another egg on the floor beside little Emma's accident. Emma looked up and said, "It's okay 'cause even adults make mistakes sometimes, Nana Gracie. I will help you clean this mess up." Grace loved her special moments in life, and this was definitely one of them.

As Grace watched Emma eating her homemade choco-late chip cookie with her freshly polished pinky nail extended, she smiled and thanked God for this darling little girl. She was reminded of how we can have so much pain in this beautiful life, but the pure innocence of one of God's little ones brings just as much joy in the midst of it. The love of a child must be God's sign of better days just moments away. A child is our hope for future peace, contentment, and happiness.

After a long and very busy day, it was time for Grace to have some relaxation. While she always loved her time with Emma and Joshy and desperately wanted to help Melissa, she was sure God knew her well when He blessed her with all of her children in her twenties.

Chapter Ten

SCATTERED MEMORIES

AS GRACE WATCHED THE STEAMY HOT WATER FLOW into her garden tub filled with the fabulous fragrance of lavender and rosemary bath salts, her mind began to drift. She had always been such a happy wife and mother. She was so thankful for her amazing husband and beautiful children. Grace was sure she had been blessed far more than any woman deserved in this life. She never took anything for granted. She was more than aware of just how quickly life can change. Grace had always been determined to embrace life and be thankful for every moment God would bless her with.

Still, she couldn't help but wonder how different her life could have been. Grace was sure most women must have these thoughts from time to time. This must surely be normal in life. She was thankful to count herself as one of the many women who always felt happy and content after visiting this part of her memory safe.

As she slipped into the hot bath and felt the bath salts start to soothe her exhausted body, she allowed the relaxation to take over her thoughts again. Grace allowed her mind to drift slowly, calmly. She wondered where her life would have taken her if she had listened to her pageant judges from years gone by. Grace was in dental hygiene school during some of her pageants. She especially loved getting scholarship money from them. This really helped her with her college expenses, and she was proud to do her part along with the help from her parents. But it was one of her huge pageants she remembered well. Grace was a singer and loved singing country gospel music. The pageant judges had strongly suggested Grace go to Nashville Tennessee and find out where her talent might take her. Grace had been a very sheltered and naïve nineteen-year-old in a small reserved town. Just the thought of the judges even suggesting this thrilled her.

Still, she knew she had her education to think about. She knew the thoughts of leaving college to pursue a career in singing country music in Nashville was beyond her comprehension. She explained this to the judges and assumed they would completely agree with her concerns. She was shocked when one of the judges replied, "I am also a college professor and I always encourage people to get their education. However, in this case, I would strongly encourage you to take a break from college and take on Nashville. Girl, you can sing." Grace was stunned! She just knew the judges would appreciate her concern for higher education. Despite the fact that singing in Nashville as a chosen career was both exciting and terrifying, Grace felt she needed to take the more mature path, or at least the safer one.

Grace did take the path of education and never had any regrets. She earned her degree in dental hygiene and was so pleased when the president of her college asked her to sing during their college graduation ceremony. He had heard Grace had written a song for her class and had performed for their individual ceremony. When he asked her to sing for their college commencement, Grace felt her desire for education and her love for singing had finally united.

Only God Above Really Knows

When we first met, we were complete strangers
We wondered then what life might have in store
Now that we have come this far together
We ask ourselves if life can give us more.

Now that we have come this far we'll keep on going
Life cannot exist without our goals
Now that we have come this far we'll keep on going
But what our future holds, only God above really knows.

As the song continued to play on in her mind, Grace could feel herself back on the huge stage. She could feel the love from her classmates and the audience as she shared her country twang through song. It was a song she had written from her heart. People loved it so much they had suggested she should get a copyright on her work. Grace took their advice and has always been proud of this accomplishment. The copyright reminds her of a time long ago when she was successful in combining her desire for education and her passion for singing.

After this wonderful experience, Grace realized she could enjoy both working in a dental office and her love for country gospel music. She didn't go to Nashville, but she continued singing in church. She especially enjoyed singing on a local Christian television station. She always felt that if God would use her to bless just one person through song, she must continue singing.

One of her best memories happened after church one beautiful afternoon. A very nice gentleman came up to Grace and thanked her for singing for them and asked her to continue. When Grace thanked him for his kind words and started to explain about the life of a very busy wife and mother of such a large family, the gentleman said, "Forgive me for interrupting, but I must say this. I wanted to be saved, and I knew God was speaking to me. I have been gripping my seat and holding on tight. Then, I heard you sing your song, and I let go." Being a former football player from years gone by, he was a very tall, big man. With tears in his eyes, he made Grace understand. God had answered her prayers, for which Grace was thankful. She now understood God would use her as His instrument to reach His children. While this would never be even the possibility of money and fame in Nashville, this was something so much more. This was her path, and Grace was so glad she had taken it.

"Are you in there?" Grace could feel her memories slipping back into the corners of her mind as she slowly opened her eyes. "Are you in there?" Grace looked up to see her gold chandelier with the lights dim. She could smell the lavender and rosemary and knew her garden tub was still hugging her with love, peace, and relaxation. "Are you still in there? Why are you taking so long?"

Grace realized the soft little whisper near her door was her sweet Emma. "Yes, Emma. I am still in my bubble bath, sweetie. I promise I will be finished very soon."

Emma answered, "I think you have been in there long enough, and I want to cuddle with you, Nana Gracie."

This made Grace smile and hurry. After all, cuddle time with Emma was relaxing too. As she stepped out of her relaxing bath, she was once again reminded she had taken the right path and she smiled with gratitude.

Chapter Eleven

TELL ME A STORY

As Grace and Emma curled up in their blanket to cuddle, Emma asked her to tell her a story. Grace always enjoyed this time together. Emma would always ask for the same story. This was a story about a little girl named Princess Emma. She was a little girl who lived in a big house up high on a big hill. Emma had asked Grace to tell this same invented story so many times that Grace decided to write a book about it.

Once Upon a Time … There Was a Big House on a Big Hill
Once upon a time
There was a little girl
Her name was
Princess Emma Grace.
Princess Emma Grace lived in a BIG house
Up high on a BIG hill.
She had a BIG brother.
His name was Prince Joshy.
He loved his baby sister
And, he also loved to play soccer.
Princess Emma Grace and Prince Joshy

Lived with their mother in the BIG house on the BIG hill.
Her name was Queen Mommy.
They all lived with their Pops and Nana Gracie
In the BIG house on the BIG hill.
They were all very happy and loved each other very much,
But sometimes they missed the rest of their BIG wonderful family.
Princess Emma, Grace, and Prince Joshy
Always looked so forward to the special days
When their other family members came to see them.
On some days
Auntie Elizabeth would visit and play with them.
On some days
Uncle Frankie would visit and sing to them.
On some days
Uncle Zachariah and Auntie Cyndirella would visit them
And bring their dog, Mokie, and their bunny, Leeroy, to play with them.
On some days
Auntie Brooke would visit them and bring their wonderful cousins to play with them.
They always had fun with Brad, Paige, Jay, and little McKenna.
On some days
Auntie Leigh would visit them and bring their sweet cousin, Brianna to play with them.
All of the royal family loved each other very much.
And they loved spending time together.
The royal family would swim together.
They would eat delicious food from the grill together.
They would celebrate so many happy birthdays together.
They always loved to celebrate Christmas together
As a family.

Sometimes they even went to the beach together for family vacations.

Princess Emma Grace loved her Daddy.

He called her every single day.

She loved their special time together.

They loved going to the park to play.

God Bless the Wonderful Royal Family ...

Love and Prayers

Nana Gracie

THE END

"Read it again, Nana Gracie!" While Grace was thrilled that her little Emma loved her book, she also knew her Sweet Baby Girl Angel Kisses needed to go off to dreamland. As she carried her to her room, Emma softly whispered, "I love you, Nana Gracie, and I promise I will come back."

Chapter Twelve

THE DREAM

As Grace walked back to her own room, she couldn't help but wonder about her life's journey. Emma had become such a precious part of her life. Grace knew all children were blessings from God above. It didn't matter to Grace exactly how the precious children had made their way into her life. She was just forever thankful they had.

As she lay her head on her pillow, she thanked God for her loving husband and wonderful children. She thanked Him for her sweet grandchildren and the many answered prayers in her life. She thanked Him for her loving parents and extended family she had been so blessed with. Above all, Grace thanked God for her salvation. As she started to give in to her much-needed rest, she heard her husband softly whisper, "I love and cherish you, Grace, and I am so thankful you are my wife. Thank you for always taking such good care of all of our children and grandchildren. Elizabeth is right. You are the glue holding our entire family together, and I appreciate you more than you will ever know." His loving words were all she needed to carry her throughout her journey. Grace fell asleep knowing she was loved and cherished beyond measure.

"Everything will be okay, Sissy … try not to worry. God will take care of you, and I will watch over you. I am always with you, and I will never leave you." Grace could see her sweet grandmother smiling as she spoke such kind words. Grace had always been so close to her grandmother. She had known only unconditional love and comfort from her. Her grandmother had been a devout Christian her entire life, and Grace was sure heaven had gained an angel. "I have been watching over you during so many difficult times, Sissy. Things will be okay. Have faith, sweet girl. God will never forsake you." Grace could feel the warmth of her grandmother's arms wrapped around her as she opened her eyes. She was overwhelmed by the visit from her loving grandmother. Could this really have been just a dream? No—this was as real as her husband sleeping beside her. Her grandmother knew Grace needed her. Just as she had many times before, she came to her in her dreams. She came to bring love, peace, and hope. She visited her dreams to comfort Grace and remind her of her own strength and faith.

As Grace stared at the ceiling unable to sleep now, she started to think of the many loved ones who had left this world. Not only had Grace taken care of her terminally ill brother-in-law when he lived in her home, but she had taken care of her mother-in-law as well. She was a very kind and soft-spoken lady. Grace loved her very much. They had grown extremely close over the years, and taking care of her during her illness came natural to Grace. After all, not only did Grace adore her, but she was also her husband's mother and her children's grandmother. As far as Grace was concerned, there was only one thing to do: the right thing. While she didn't live in their home with Grace and her husband, Grace would spend a lot of time going to her so she could help. It didn't really matter if it was in her mother-in-law's home or in a hospital; they always enjoyed their visits. Grace loved their many talks and was more than thankful for their relationship. She had once told Grace she was more like a daughter to her than a daughter-in-law, and Grace knew she would forever cherish this. She would always tell Grace she had taken her breath away on the day of her wedding when she vowed "to love and to cherish" her son. She said it was the heartfelt way her daughter-in-law had said "cherish." She knew she had nothing to worry about because her son had finally found true happiness in life, and she was so grateful.

It was a cold, snowy day when God called her home. The loss of her mother-in-law was very difficult for Grace. She felt as though her heart had suffered a hit-and-run accident. The pain her husband had to endure was almost more than Grace could take. She would never forget how kind her family, friends, and neighbors had been. Her own parents had driven back and forth from Kentucky throughout her mother-in-law's illness to be of help. Grace knew she could not have endured this without them. Her parents were very close to her husband's parents, and Grace had always been so pleased. Grace also couldn't help but notice how loving and kind her father-in-law and his wife had been. Grace appreciated their kindness. Despite things not working out for her mother-in-law and father-in-law many years ago, they had been blessed with a beautiful family during their years together, and this needed to be respected. Grace admired her in-laws for showing such love and compassion during this difficult time. Grace was also glad to have her own brothers, sister-in-law, and her beautiful Aunt June during this time of such sorrow. Grace came from a family of deep love and concern for each other. She knew she could always count on them. They adored her husband and always had. Grace was thankful that they knew him well and loved him so much.

As Grace continued to toss and turn, she kept thinking about her sweet mother-in-law. Grace still missed her every single day. The day of her funeral brought with it the blizzard of 1993. Grace and her family were shocked to find out there would be no burial following the funeral due to the blizzard. Her lovely mother-in-law would be laid to rest exactly seven days later. The snow was still deep, and life in their hometown had come to a complete stop. The family had decided that due to the snow and unsafe road conditions, they would allow the funeral director to take care of the burial. After all, they had already gone through the pain and grief of saying their goodbyes during the funeral service a week earlier. They had been through so much for an entire week searching for some sort of closure. Their comfort came from knowing she was in heaven now and no longer suffering.

Grace was home with her children while the schools were closed due to the blizzard. Her husband was at work, and his sister was as well. Grace could still remember being home and wishing she could go to the cemetery. She couldn't allow her mother-in-law to be there without any family. After leaving her children with her in-laws next door, Grace headed out on the ice-covered roads. She prayed God would take her there safely and bring her back to her children. She just knew her husband would be so pleased she had gone to be with his mother once he knew she was back home safe. When she arrived, there stood her husband and her sweet sister-in-law. They each smiled at each other because none of them had kept their promise to avoid the unsafe road conditions. They simply held hands and said goodbye to their precious mother … for now.

By now, Grace was exhausted from her lack of sleep. It had just been one of those nights. She felt as though she had been working night shift, and her job was the keeper of the clock. Just as the sun started to shine through her bedroom window, she heard her phone ringing. It was her husband's stepmother; his dad was ill. As Grace was getting ready to go to the hospital, she prayed. Could this have been the reason her grandmother came to her in her dream? Was this what she meant by saying everything would be okay? Grace wondered if God had used her grandmother to help prepare her family for something. She continued to pray without ceasing.

As Grace stayed by her father-in-law's bedside in the hospital, so many memories came flooding back. Grace and her husband had lived next door to him for over twenty years of their long marriage. They had raised their children next door to their grandfather. He loved having his son and his family just a few steps away in life. Grace adored her father-in-law, and he adored her as well. He would always let her know how proud he was of her as a wife and mother and that he was beyond happy with his daughter-in-law.

He and Grace shared a love of flowers. Every time he would see her tending to her flower gardens, he had to walk over to investigate. He had taught Grace so much about her flowers, and she was so appreciative. Grace would never plant her first flower in the spring until he gave her both green thumbs-up. More than anything, he taught her to love her flowers. He would remind her of their responsibility to take care of all living things. This included her flowerbeds. He believed God sent both the sun and the rain as free tools for us to use on earth. Grace was always thrilled to use a watering can she had strategically placed to catch the rain to water her flowers. This always pleased her sweet father-in-law because he knew he had taught her well. Flowers and gardening had become their thing. It was something they shared and both had a passion for. He would bring her fresh tomatoes and delicious cucumbers from his own garden. In return, she would share starts from her beautiful flowers. Together, they worked hard in their yards and lived on their lovely lane as both neighbors and family for over twenty years.

This once very strong and energetic man looked so helpless to Grace now. She had only seen him look broken a few times over the years. Once was when he found out Zachariah had cancer. He was a tough grandfather, but this had devastated him. He couldn't stop working in their yard when Grace and her husband were with their son in Mayo Clinic. Taking care of their yard was his way of doing something for them. Grace knew it was his "thinking time" as well. Her father-in-law, who she lovingly called "Papaw," was from the "old school" in life. He didn't make appointments with a wonderful doctor and pay for therapy. He worked with his hands and used this time to think things through. This always worked for him, and his long life was proof of this.

As Grace continued to stay by his bedside in the hospital, her mind continued to drift back over the years. She had such a beautiful history with him, and their lives had been put together like a wonderful puzzle. Grace knew each puzzle piece had found its place to fit just right. He had served his country and loved his family, but he would never really get over the loss of his eldest son. Grace would never forget the last moments with her sweet brother-in-law. The family couldn't understand what was taking Papaw so long to walk over. After all, they lived on the same short lane. Then, he came through the bedroom door. His body was trembling, and he was obviously shaken. He knelt beside his eldest son and held his hand. Grace would never forget what he said as he softly whispered, "I'm so sorry I took so long, son. I was lowering my flag to honor you. You served our great country, and you deserve it. I'm so proud of you, and I love you, son."

71

As her sweet brother-in-law was carried away and taken from her home, Grace knew her family had been changed forever. She thanked God for allowing them to be there for one of His precious lambs. She knew in her heart they would be stronger as a family having helped a fellow human being during his last moments on this earth. She was so thankful to know he felt so loved by so many at the end of his life.

There was a chill in the air as the family gathered on the banks of the Greenbrier River to say goodbye to her brother-in-law. Grace knew this would be a difficult day for her husband. The loss of his big brother had broken his heart. But he knew he had a job to do. His brother had asked him to spread his ashes in the Greenbrier River. This was a place in the gorgeous mountains of West Virginia where they had run and played as children. It was a place where they had gone fishing and shared their childhood secrets. They had gone swimming on the glistening rapids without a care in the world. Here on the Greenbrier River, they had been invincible and would live forever. Everyone more than understood why he would want to return to his childhood paradise. As her husband spoke of his only brother, prayed, and explained his last wishes, Grace felt a peace all around them. As he spread his brother's ashes and asked God to take care of him now, the sun glistened through the trees and bounced off the river like dancing angels. Each and every family member placed a rose in the river and watched as the roses found their way to him. He floated away with his beautiful childhood memories in his favorite river and the healing began.

"Honey, I think I might need a nurse."

Grace was brought back to reality when she heard her father-in-law speak. Her memories would have to slip back into the corners of her mind for now until she had a chance to visit them again. "I'm here, Papaw," she said, smiling.

"Oh, I knew you would be, Grace." His voice sounded weak, and Grace just wanted to do something to help him. She asked him why he needed a nurse, and he explained that he was hungry. Just as Grace started to ask for something, his breakfast arrived. In his frail voice, he said he thought he needed a nurse to help him.

Grace smiled and said, "I don't think so, Papaw. I would be more than pleased to help my father-in-law with his breakfast." She placed his napkin on his chest and started spoon-feeding her sweet father-in-law one bite after another until his breakfast was gone, along with his hunger. He smiled and thanked her for being there for him and said he might need to rest now. He asked Grace if she would still be there when he woke up. She replied, "I'm not going anywhere, Papaw. I promise I will be right here when you wake up." He smiled as he drifted off again. He knew she would keep her promise to him because she always had.

They were blessed to have Papaw for a little while after this. God called him home a year later. He didn't suffer, and Grace was so grateful for this. She knew this was his biggest fear after watching his eldest son suffer so much with cancer. His precious heart gave out and he simply went to sleep. Grace knew he would open his eyes in heaven to see his own parents and siblings with his precious son waiting for him. She was sure they would fish together and never suffer again. This brought Grace and her entire family so much comfort.

Now Grace needed to help her husband heal once again. She had been with him through the loss of his mother, his only brother, and now his father. Grace knew their faith would see them through this, but she also knew her husband was hurting, and she needed to be there for him. More than ever before, she was so thankful she had been so close to her father-in-law. She knew in her heart that this brought comfort to her husband and would be a huge part of his own healing. For this, Grace gave God the glory.

Chapter Thirteen

SPRING FLOWERS

AS TIME MARCHED ON AND THE SEASONS BEGAN TO change, Grace often thought of her father-in-law. She knew if she missed him this much, her husband must have missed him beyond words. It was now spring, and Grace longed to hear his voice again. She missed his two green thumbs and gardening expertise. Most of all, she missed his gentle way of encouraging her in life. They were much more than father-in-law and daughter-in-law. They were friends. He had a way of bringing out the "old soul" in Grace. She loved this easy feeling of calmness and feeling so connected to nature while tending her flowers. They would spend hours in her potting shed, and she had learned so much from him. She couldn't help but wish he had taught her how to let go before leaving her. Then one day while planting her new yellow day-lilies, she realized something. Papaw was in every flower she planted. He was smiling from each and every yellow bloom, and she felt his very presence as she cultivated the rich soil. As she looked around, she realized he was with her throughout her beautiful flower gardens. He had not com-pletely left her because he left behind a beautiful part of his sweet soul. He had managed to sprinkle reminders of their gardening together and a promise of their everlasting connection. Grace knew Papaw would be with her forever. She knew she would never see a beautiful flower again without thinking of her sweet father-in-law. God had brought their paths together during her life's journey, and Grace was so grateful for this. Grace knew she had been so very blessed to have wonderful parents in this life. She felt beyond blessed to also have been given the beautiful gift of such loving in-laws as well.

This beautiful connection to her flower garden reminded Grace of something her own mother had always said. Despite the fact Grace never wanted to even think about the day she might lose her own parents, she understood her mother better now. Her mother would always say God would take her home someday. She said when this happens, don't be sad and just know she was in a better place. She would always smile and say, "Just look for me in the butterflies. When you see a butterfly, you will know I am near." After connecting with Papaw in the garden, Grace now understood. She believed in her heart, God helps our loved ones watch over us and allows them to give us a sign to let us feel their presence. They let us know they are near, which brings much-needed comfort and healing.

As Grace finished planting her daylilies, she once again found herself on her knees, and she began to pray. She often prayed while in her garden. This was always the perfect meeting place for her to bring her prayers to God. After all, the garden was such a peaceful place of nature. She couldn't help but be reminded of all His beautiful creations while she was in this place. As she brought her burdens and all her worries to God, she never forgot to thank Him for her many blessings. Grace understood she couldn't only call on God when she was in need. She must always thank Him for all He has given her in this life. On this day, she thanked him for her wonderful husband and her beautiful children. She thanked Him for her grandchildren and her entire family. She thanked God for providing her a life with wonderful parents and brothers. She always asked God to forgive her of her mistakes as a Christian. She asked Him to help her be a better Christian wife and mother—a better Christian woman. On this day, Grace thanked God for bringing Papaw to the garden. She thanked Him for giving her this understanding and allowing her to feel his presence. As she felt the sun on her face, she thanked Him for never forsaking her. Grace thanked Him for the many answered prayers in her life. She praised Him for allowing her son to survive cancer. She thanked him for bringing both of her parents through such serious health issues. She sobbed as she remembered her dad on life support and praised God he was saved following this ordeal at the age of eighty-two. She thanked God for bringing her mom through a serious and very long health scare. She knew with everything in her, she had known times of such sorrow, but her faith had carried her. God stayed with her during every painful moment. He had listened to her and had never left her. Grace didn't need to see His divine face to be sure. Through His grace and her unshaken faith, Grace just knew. God was always there for her, and she was eternally grateful.

"Baby doll, don't you think it's too hot outside to be doing this right now?" Grace looked up to see her husband standing above her. As she squinted to see him better with the sun in her eyes, she could see him holding something. He had the most beautiful bouquet of flowers and the sweetest smile to go with them. He said he saw the flowers and thought of his wife. Grace leaped to her feet and threw her arms around his neck. He knew she loved flowers and was always thrilled to get them. As she looked down at the gorgeous rainbow bouquet, the colors and fragrance took her breath away. Just as she was reminded of the many times her sweet father-in-law had surprised her with freshly cut flowers, something else caught her eyes. The florist had included three beautiful silk butterflies throughout the gorgeous bouquet. When her husband asked her what she was thinking about, she answered, "I'm just thinking about how blessed I am to have such an amazing and thoughtful husband." Grace knew she was thinking much more than this; her heart was overflowing with emotion. But these were her very own thoughts and a sign from God about life.

For now, she would hug her husband and show him just how much she appreciated his love and thoughtfulness. This was their moment, and Grace was so thankful. Her husband just smiled and said, "I realize we may not be ready to retire yet and spend our days walking hand in hand on the beach gathering seashells, but for now, I can still bring you flowers."

Grace and her husband looked forward to the day when they would live on the beach. They both loved walking on the beach and gathering seashells. They especially loved the beach during the offseason. Grace loved to relax in a beach chair with her husband by her side as the ocean washed over their feet. They loved leaving their sliding glass door open and falling asleep to the sound of the waves crashing over the sand, washing the day away so they could start all over again the following morning. It was as though the ocean had created a clean slate with fresh sand, leaving behind all new treasures for them to find each new day. They couldn't move there yet, but they would someday. With her husband's heart condition, this move to paradise couldn't come soon enough for Grace. She always said she didn't need things. She only needed more precious time with her husband. For now, they would love each other and enjoy the small things in life.

As she and her husband gathered her gardening tools to go inside, Grace smiled. There in the middle of her beautiful flower garden among the many bright yellow daylilies, Grace knew she was the luckiest woman in the world. As she gathered her beautiful bouquet from her husband, she took time to smell the flowers and once again, she thanked God. After all, she had been blessed with a beautiful day of gardening and her husband had surprised her with flowers. What more could a woman need in life?

Chapter Fourteen

THE HEART OF A LITTLE BOY

IT WAS GETTING LATE, AND GRACE WAS EXHAUSTED from her long day of gardening when she heard a knock on her bedroom door. It was her sweet little guy Joshy. "May I come in, Nana Gracie?"

Grace replied, "Of course you may come in, sweetie. What do you need, Joshy?"

He answered in his sleepy voice, "Emma said you always read to her when I am in school and I don't think it's very fair to me. She said you always read her special book to her. I'm talking about the one you wrote for her."

Grace smiled as she answered, "I do read to Emma when you are in school. Joshy, I do many things with her while I am babysitting for your mommy. Why do you feel this is unfair to you, sweetie? I'm a little confused."

Joshy just smiled as he replied, "Well, I just think you should read the book you wrote for me, too. You haven't read it to me in a long time, and it's not really fair." Grace smiled as she told him to run to his room and get his special book. She then laughed when he pulled the book from behind his little back.

As they cuddled up together to share a story, Grace knew these were the moments she would cherish forever.

A Story about My High Energy
Sweet and Loving
Little Guy Joshy

There once was a little boy.
Joshy was his name.
He brought his family so much joy.
Life was just a game.

Joshy loved to run and play.
His energy was off the charts.
He rode his bike and kicked the ball.
Sometimes he played with darts.

Joshy really loved to hike and fish.
He even became a scout.
He also really loved to swim.
He loved to jump and shout.

Joshy loved his mother with all of his heart.
He thought she hung the moon in the sky.
He knew she was beautiful, kind, and smart.
Joshy knew he was her sweet little guy.

Joshy did not have a little brother.
Instead, he had a baby sister.
He really loved her like no other.
When not together, he always missed her.

Joshy loved spaghetti, pizza and lots of chicken.

But he mostly wanted to eat sweets.
His mom would say NO to his lollipop licking.
It was dinner first and then his treats.

Joshy loved to play so many sports,
But soccer was his game.
He kicked the ball both long and short
Under the sun or in the rain.

Joshy was a little guy with a great big family,
He loved all of his relatives very much.
He would share his hugs so lovingly
He was thankful for their tender touch.

Joshy really did not like his timeout chair,
But he did love to catch creepy things.
Sometimes he liked to change his hair.
Joshy never forgot to wear sunscreen.

Joshy really loved his dad.
He knew his dad was big and strong.
His dad was his very own hero.
Joshy just knew he could do no wrong.

This was the story of a little boy named Joshy.
Love and Prayers, Nana Gracie

As Grace closed the book, she asked Joshy if he had enjoyed his special story all about him. With a little grin, he said, "I love my book all about me, and I sure bet you feel better now, Nana Gracie."

Grace replied, "I love to read to you, but I'm not exactly sure what you are talking about, Joshy."

As he put his little arms around her neck and hugged her, he whispered, "I'm just pretty sure you have been missing me and spending time with me. You know how you are about stuff like that, Nana Gracie."

Grace felt his little arms hugging her so tight, and as always, he had once again managed to pull on her heart-strings. She whispered in his little ear, "You know me very well, Joshy. I have been missing our special time together, and I love you very much!" She tickled his tummy and teased, "Why do I love you so much? You are not my kid!"

Joshy giggled and answered in his high pitch squeal, "Because you are my Nana Gracie!" Grace smiled and held his little hand all the way to his bedroom. As she tucked him in and promised to leave his nightlight on until his mommy arrived, she reminded him it was time to say his prayers.

God bless my mom ...
God bless my dad ...
God Bless my baby sister ...
God bless my Pops ...
God bless my Nana Gracie ...
God bless my Auntie Elizabeth ...
God bless my Uncle Frankie ...
God bless my Uncle Zachariah ...
God bless my Auntie Cyndirella ...
God bless my Auntie Leigh and Briana ...
God bless my Auntie Brooke and Mal ...
God bless Brad and Paige and Jay and McKenna ...
God bless my Nanny and Poppy in Kentucky ...
God bless my Nanny Charlotte and Papaw in heaven ...
God bless all my other grandparents and family and friends ...
Oh! I almost forgot!

Thank You, God, for everything …
AMEN.

Grace loved his tender heart and his long and loving prayer. She tucked him in and turned on his nightlight. Just as she started to leave his room, he yelled, "I have a great idea, Nana Gracie! I think from now on when I say my prayer I will just say something like 'Thank You God for everything and God bless my whole family!'"

Grace smiled and said she thought this would be a wonderful idea. Joshy replied, *"Thank goodness, because our family is huge, and I get a little bit tired."*

As Grace kissed him on the forehead, she thanked God for bringing this little boy into her life. Having raised two precious sons of her own, she understood the tender heart of a little boy. As she walked back to her own bedroom, Grace took a slight detour. She often loved to relax on the couch in her formal living room. Her favorite spot was next to a sliding glass door. Because of the full-length glass windows on each side of the door, the entire wall opened up to the outside, allowing a spectacular view. She especially loved to relax in this space when the rest of her family was sleeping and their home was filled with silence.

As she curled up on the couch with her favorite cozy blanket from Elizabeth and a nice hot cup of chamomile tea, Grace thought about her two wonderful sons. Zachariah and Frankie were both college graduates now and fine young men. They both had hearts the size of Texas! While Grace was more than thankful for this, she often thought about the little boys brought into this world to steal her heart. Her sons had always been close. They were little partners in crime throughout their childhood. Zachariah was the eldest and full of energy. He was more than happy to be the fierce leader on their many adventures. Frankie was the calm younger brother, and he was always willing to follow. As a mother, she always enjoyed overhearing them in the midst of childhood playtime. Zachariah would be making an elaborate plan, and he would be giving Frankie his detailed instructions about his plan. Frankie would be hanging on his big brother's every word in hopes of doing his part in completing their mission. They were always there for each other. When Grace would visit these precious memories, she could almost still hear their giggles and late-night whispers from the bunk beds in their childhood bedroom. She assumed they were making more plans to carry out their exciting adventures the following day. While she had many wonderful memories stored in the safe designed for her sons, one memory often came to mind.

It was a sunny afternoon, and Elizabeth had a softball game. The boys didn't really want to go to yet another game and asked Grace if they could have their good friend Jack over to play instead. Jack was a sweet boy just a few months younger than Zachariah. The boys spent every possible moment together and were more like family than neighborhood friends. Grace adored Jack, and he knew it. Still, the thoughts of these three boys and their adventures while home alone worried Grace. She and her husband needed to be with their baby daughter, so a decision had to be made. After many promises of near perfect behavior in her absence, Grace gave in. But this was under one condition! The boys had to promise they would only play inside where they would be safe. Grace knew they were old enough to spend a few hours home alone, especially knowing her in-laws and Jack's mother would be next door. Both moms were very good friends and often watched each other's children. Grace adored her sweet friend Dawn and felt loved by her as well. After the promise of inside activities only, Grace and her husband were off to the softball game. As the boys waved goodbye from their bedroom window, Grace felt secure in knowing they would be safe while having fun together.

The game had just started, and the sun was beaming down on the teams and their parents when Grace received the call on her cell phone. It was Jack, and he sounded very upset. "Jack, you need to slow down. I can't understand you. What happened?'"

Jack answered slowly, "I think you need to come home right now, Grace. I think we need to take Zachariah to the hospital."

Grace replied, "Why would we need to take him to the hospital? What in the world happened?"

He answered, "Well, I'm pretty sure he broke his arm when he fell out of the tree."

Grace could hear the panic in her own voice as she replied, "I don't understand, Jack! We don't have a tree in our house!"

She heard him say in a very slow and calm voice, "I agree, but I don't really think we have time to talk about that part right now. He is really hurting, and you'd better come home so we can take him to the hospital."

Grace knew she would never forget this conversation. It would become one of her many moments in life. She wasn't shocked when the sweet young boy from across the road went on to serve his country as his chosen career. After all, he knew how to stay calm in a crisis.

Chapter Fifteen

FATHER TIME

THE CLOCK CHIMED THREE TIMES. HAD GRACE really been looking out over the nighttime lights scattered across the small town in the distance for this long? She felt consumed by her memories of her sweet boys. Her book of memories held so many pages of happiness and comfort for Grace. Where had this precious time gone?

Grace had always felt loved by her sons. They both had a very special way of making her feel cherished and protected. She wasn't sure if this was just the natural relationship between all mothers and sons or just their very own special way of being with each other. She was only sure of the mother/son relationships she had been so very blessed with. As Grace looked out over their small hometown, she could not think of one single time either of her sons had ever spoken to her in a disrespectful way. Grace was so thankful for this cherished knowledge, and she felt sure their dad had been a wonderful role model. Zachariah and Frankie had grown up watching their dad show only love and kindness towards their mother. Grace felt sure that this had helped them be the kind and compassionate men they had become. She had been loved dearly and respected by her own dad and both of her brothers. She was thankful to know she had also been loved dearly and respected by her father-in-law, brother-in-law, husband, and both of her sons. She never took these blessings for granted. She gave God the glory for all of the wonderful men in her life on this earth.

As her mind continued to drift back over the years, she could see her children's sweet faces—each and every one of them. Her three older daughters loved to carry the three younger children around on their hips. Grace would never forget how excited her children were when their big sisters would spend time with them. She knew they had been blessed to have been together so often for so many years. Together they just had a way of completely overflowing their home with pure happiness and joy.

Grace could still see her sweet little Elizabeth spending her days chasing after her two older brothers and all of their friends. She would laugh and giggle as she won them over every single time. She was always willing to entertain them if only they would include her in their childhood adventures. Grace attempted to keep a lovely bow in Elizabeth's long, gorgeous blonde hair and made sure she had all the girly things a little girl could ask for.

But Grace knew Elizabeth's heart would forever remain with her dad on the back of his four-wheeler and fishing with him in their pond. Elizabeth would rather be climbing trees with her big brothers and hiding in their tree house on any given day. This became obvious one day while organizing Elizabeth's own special area of their toy room. As Grace started to tidy up her doll accessories and put them back in her dollhouse, she was startled. In each bedroom, Elizabeth had placed a worm on each little pink bed and put the little family people outside of the dollhouse. Most of the worms had most certainly already gone to "worm heaven," but a few still remained in their beautiful new pink and white dream home. Grace decided this was a job for her husband. After all, he had created their little bow-wearing worm lover. She simply closed the lovely front door of the beautiful dollhouse and left the new residents alone. After this, Grace was more mindful of what she might find while organizing her daughter's toys. She would do so only with caution and a smile.

Elizabeth always had a way with her brothers and their friends. While Grace knew she must have been cramping their style a little, she couldn't help but notice just how kind and accepting they were of this little girl who was trying desperately to be part of their clique. Elizabeth just knew it was a special club full of playtime and many adventures. She was determined to not only be included, but she needed to be in charge from time to time. Grace would never forget the time she found Jack all alone, just resting on the bottom of her stairs. As she looked at Jack and noticed his unhappy demeanor, she could hear all of the other children laughing and playing in the upstairs toy room. When she asked him if something was wrong, nothing could have prepared her for his answer. Jack just put his head down and replied, "Elizabeth put me in time out."

Grace was shocked as she asked, "Why on earth would Elizabeth put you in time out, Jack? Better yet, why on earth would you listen to her about this?"

Jack looked up and said, "It's okay, Grace. She is just upset because I wouldn't kiss her goofy doll. Besides, I don't have much longer." As Grace just walked away completely stunned, she overheard Jack speaking to Elizabeth. He was very firm as he said, "Okay, Elizabeth! I will kiss your goofy doll if you let me get up early and go back upstairs to play. But I am only doing this one time, and you'd better never ask me to again!"

Elizabeth replied, "Okay, Jack! Here you go ... on the lips!" As Grace attempted to sneak away before they heard her laugh, she heard a big smacking noise. She was sure this must have been Jack's very first kiss.

Despite her baby daughter fighting for her rightful place in the adventurous world surrounding her, Grace knew the boys often gave Elizabeth a difficult time. She knew she would not live long enough to forget the time she heard her baby daughter screaming from the garage. Grace ran to her as fast as her feet would take her. Being shocked was an understatement on this particular day of childhood playtime. There they were at the top of the garage stairs. Zachariah, Frankie, and Jack: all partners in crime.

Elizabeth was with them as well. She was the one the boys had decided to strap to a dolly using their good old faithful duct tape. As Elizabeth screamed for her mother's help, Grace heard Jack say with a grin, "I knew we should have put some duct tape over her mouth first."

Grace insisted on some apologies from the boys and attempted to free her daughter from her captivity as fast as she could—well, as fast as she could remove duct tape from the arms, legs, and tummy of a little girl. Grace knew in her heart that the boys never intended to hurt Elizabeth. She was sure they only wanted to include her in their fun and daring adventures. Despite this being the very thing Elizabeth wanted more than anything every single day of her precious childhood, Grace followed her motherly instincts and decided to hide the duct tape from her sons and their rambunctious friends. As usual, she did this with a smile on her face. After all, motherhood had a way of bringing many smiles to Grace's face and pure joy to her heart.

Chapter Sixteen

EARLY MORNING REFLECTION

AS GRACE SLIPPED BACK INTO HER WARM BED, SHE was careful not to wake her husband. He only had a couple hours left to rest before getting ready for work. Grace knew how hard her husband worked to provide for their huge family, and she often worried about him. After he was diagnosed with congestive heart failure, she knew they couldn't take his health for granted. She was exhausted from the lack of sleep and knew her sweet Emma would need her Nana Gracie in just a few hours. Grace listened to the sound of her husband softly breathing and thanked God for him. As the early morning light slowly made its way through the windows of their master suite, Grace could now see the scar on her husband's chest in the soft glow of the shadows bouncing off the walls. It was a reminder of just how close she had come to losing the love of her life. A pacemaker and defibrillator were now just a normal part of his body, and this was okay. God had intervened, and while Grace knew they had been blessed with wonderful physicians, she also knew God was the greatest physician of all, and she was forever thankful for His amazing grace. She now lovingly called her husband her very own bionic man.

Grace would never forget when they realized something was wrong. They had been in Hawaii for a dental convention and made sure to extend their trip so they could celebrate their twenty-fifth wedding anniversary. Despite their age difference of just over twelve years, Grace had always been so accustomed to her husband having more energy than he knew what to do with. He would do dentistry all day and spend his evenings taking care of their three gorgeous acres along the riverbank and where they raised their children. He would tend to his fishing pond and maintain a huge pool and hot tub for his family. Also, he always took his wife and children to church and worked in three or four days of golf with his wonderful friends. His energy and stamina were extremely impressive. This was who he had always been during all their years together. This was why the Hawaii trip made Grace notice something was wrong with her husband. While they were both so pleased to have had the most amazing two weeks in Hawaii, looking back on their time there, they both realized he was slowly becoming ill. He had a lot of walking to do during his dental convention, which proved to be very difficult for him.

After the convention, Grace and her husband continued their amazing stay in Hawaii to celebrate their silver anniversary. One of her favorite memories was waking up early one morning in Maui and walking out on their balcony to find her husband writing a message in the sand for her. This was better than any anniversary card he could have purchased. Grace was sure she fell in love with him all over again. They enjoyed several different islands of Hawaii and enjoyed so many different things the culture had to offer. They went hiking in the rainforest together and were absolutely amazed with its beauty. They stood beneath some of the most gorgeous waterfalls and enjoyed the most breathtaking sunsets they had ever seen. They hiked over lava rocks to see some amazing volcanoes. Here on the islands of Hawaii with all of their vibrant beauty, her husband found his inner photographer. But it was also here on the islands of Hawaii that Grace realized her husband had very little energy and was having difficulty breathing. As she noticed him holding his hand over his chest, it was obvious his breathing was labored. Combined with his low energy, this made her heart sank. Grace could not believe how strikingly similar her husband's symptoms were to their son's cancer. Grace was terrified, but her husband never knew this. She knew once again she needed to brace herself because somebody she loved was very ill and would need her to be strong.

Once they returned home, Grace was sure her husband's symptoms were much worse. He made an appointment with his primary physician. Grace was more than concerned when she realized her husband had been given an inhaler for asthma just as their son had before they took him to a doctor who was known for his diagnostic skills. As his symptoms continued to get worse, Grace was getting very worried. She knew the inhaler wasn't helping her husband any more than an inhaler had helped her son while he was suffering with cancer. She was so happy when her husband took it upon himself to ask his doctor to refer him to a cardiologist. Grace had no idea what their future held concerning her husband's health issues. She only knew he needed her by his side, and her faith would take care of the rest.

Grace would never forget this early morning appointment with her husband. She could still remember holding his hand as they anxiously waited to see the cardiologist. There were so many possibilities of what this might be. It was almost more than Grace could take, but she knew her husband needed her to stay strong. She continued to hold his hand, smile lovingly, and pray. After all, her husband and family had always been able to depend on Grace during their most difficult times. This was who she was. She was and always had been a strong woman of faith. Grace knew her husband was the love of her entire life. She knew he was the very best part of her, and he just had to be well. Grace also knew they had lost a certain innocence after their son's illness. She more than understood that life wasn't always fair. Still, Grace was a fighter. She didn't give up easily. Her wonderful husband and amazing children always knew they could depend on her to be in their corner. Above everything else, Grace was a determined prayer warrior. She often said she wondered if God had a special committee of angels watching over her huge family because of her many prayers. Grace was always so grateful for her many answered prayers. Most of all, she was thankful that she always remembered to give God the glory.

Grace could feel her husband grip her hand much tighter as his cardiologist entered the room. As his doctor looked over his medical records and glanced back and forth at them, it was obvious he seemed concerned. Grace could feel her heart pounding when he finally spoke to her husband. "Have you been having symptoms a long time? I'm asking because I am shocked to see just how well you seem to be functioning considering what the tests have revealed." Then the doctor said those words Grace knew would change their lives forever. He explained her husband had congestive heart failure and his heart was in really bad shape. Grace felt numb as she continued to hold the strongest hand she had ever known. As the doctor continued explaining the diagnosis, she could feel their hands tremble. Grace wasn't sure if it was her hand or her husband's causing them to tremble. She only knew they needed each other now more than ever, and she was determined to be his strength.

Grace found herself silently praying on the drive home when she felt her husband take her hand in his. He immediately started trying to comfort her and ease her worry as he always had in their years together. He reminded her of the many trials they had faced together in life and how blessed they were to have God to turn to during life's struggles. How could he be thinking of her while he was the very one facing this health crisis? Grace knew the answer before she even had time to think about the question. They were truly one in this life together and shared everything as one. This meant the amazing times as well as the most difficult times life has to offer. He squeezed her hand and told her he loved her more than anything in this world. He thanked her for making his life more than he ever dreamed it could be. Grace felt the tears streaming down her face and as they gently fell onto their clutching hands, she whispered softly, "Please don't ever leave me ... I can't be on this earth without you."

As they pulled up to their lovely home, they noticed Zachariah's little red truck in their driveway. They weren't expecting him, but they weren't surprised. Grace had sent a mass family text explaining what they had been told because they knew all of their children had been very worried about their dad. As they walked through the front door, they found their eldest son going through mounds of research papers on their dining room table. He had already started his in-depth study on his dad's congestive heart failure diagnosis. Being his mother, Grace knew her son was very concerned. The seriousness of his tone was somewhat unnerving to her. His dad attempted to make light of the situation because he did not want his son upset and worried, but Zachariah wasn't having it. He demanded his dad listen carefully to all he had learned in his research and understand just how serious the diagnosis was. Both Grace and her husband were well aware of the seriousness of congestive heart failure. It broke their hearts to see their son this worried and upset. Then Zachariah said something they would never forget. Grace could hear the pain in her son's voice as he explained, "Dad, congestive heart failure is extremely serious, with a life expectancy of five years. Hopefully longer with various treatments involving medications, a pacemaker, and a defibrillator. Some patients may even require a heart transplant. Dad, you were willing to go to the ends of the earth to save me from a rare cancer. Now, we really need you to fight just as hard for your own health. Let me help you."

With tears in his eyes and realizing their roles had reversed, Grace's husband promised his son he would fight this and do whatever he had to do to take care of his health. They would face this together as a family. Zachariah held his dad to this promise and was with him every step of the way as his dad had been there for him.

Grace was so thankful to have all six of her children surrounding her as the cardiologist performed the procedure in the very early hours on that cold, crisp morning. Words could never describe how relieved she was once the doctor explained the pacemaker and defibrillator had been a success. The cardiologist was a personal friend, and he had been extremely concerned about the possibility of sudden death occurring before he had a chance to do this procedure. He could not wait to give Grace the wonderful news, and Grace felt blessed beyond measure. Once again, God was the greatest physician, and He had wrapped His healing arms around someone Grace cherished. Her faith had once again sustained her. It had carried her when she was unable to find the strength to walk alone. As Grace stayed by her husband's hospital bed that night, she praised God for all He had continued to bless them with. She praised God as she watched her husband resting. She thanked Him for gathering her six children by her side earlier and taking them home safely so she could have this special time to give God the glory. Grace was thankful to know she would be taking her husband home the next day so they could start life together taking care of their huge family of blessings with a much healthier patriarch to lead them on life's journey.

Chapter Seventeen

THEY LEFT THEIR
HEART PRINTS BEHIND

As Grace felt the early morning sky starting to open up, she heard a soft knocking on her bedroom door. "Are you ready for me yet, Nana Gracie?" It was the sweet voice of her tiny Emma ready to start her day. Grace had enjoyed starting her day with little Emma for over four-and-a-half years now that Emma had celebrated her fifth birthday in her home. The bond they shared was something Grace had never expected, but knew she would cherish forever.

Both Joshy and Emma had brought so much joy to Grace and her husband. They filled their home with love in its purest form. Grace never imagined she could fall so deeply in love with these precious children, but she adored them and thanked God for the opportunity to be there for them during these most important formative years. While Grace had always looked forward to starting her days with little Emma, she knew today was different. Emma's mommy had met someone new and was engaged now. They were moving out and starting their new and exciting adventure in life. Lee was a wonderful man, and it was clear to Grace and her husband just how much he loved their eldest daughter and adored their precious grandchildren. Grace was so happy for all of them, but she also knew this would be a very difficult time for both her and her husband. She understood life brings with it many seasons, and while she was beyond happy for their daughter and her sweet young family, Grace also knew part of her heart was breaking. She took a deep breath and prayed for strength as she planned to make sure both Emma and Joshy would enjoy their moving day with all the excitement they were anticipating. Grace choked back the tears. With her Nana Gracie smile, she opened the door to her sweet, smiling Emma.

"I think I need you to hold me today, Nana Gracie," Emma said, looking up with the sweetest expression. Grace was determined to put her youngest granddaughter first and never let her see the pain she was feeling. She simply scooped her up into her arms and started dancing around the room to their favorite tunes. They both danced and giggled to the music until Emma finally fell asleep in her Nana Gracie's loving arms. Grace watched Emma sleep, trying to take in every precious moment. She listened carefully as Emma softly breathed in and out, reminding Grace of the years she had spent holding her while she slept. As she held her in her arms, she thought back over the many moments they had shared together. She was reminded of some very important days as well as the everyday things involved while simply doing life together.

Grace knew she was so blessed to have celebrated Emma's first five birthdays in her home and so many beautiful memories to last forever from the many Christmas and Easter mornings. Grace was there with opened arms when Emma took her very first steps beside the front door. Nana Gracie had potty-trained Joshy and watched both children start their very first day of school. Grace remembered the time Emma had given them a scare when she had been hospitalized. This reminded her of the time little Joshy had broken his arm and was so brave wearing his cast. He wore it like a badge of honor with a huge smile. Other less eventful days had been just as precious to Grace because they would remain in her heart forever. These were the days that created the bond they had come to know and love so deeply. Grace continued to hold Emma and sing her favorite song to her while she was resting in her arms.

Go to sleepy,
Go to sleepy.
Go to sleep, baby girl.
I will hold you.
Nana Gracie loves you.
You are so precious in this world.

As Grace continued stroking Emma's cheek and singing softly, she opened her little eyes and whispered, "I love you so much, Nana Gracie." This melted Grace's heart as she told Emma she loved her to the moon and back forever! Emma smiled and asked, "Will you promise me you will let me know if you and Pops ever move from this house, Nana Gracie? Will you promise you will give me your new address if you do move, Nana Gracie?" This absolutely took Grace's breath away as she searched for just the right words of comfort. She was determined to put Emma's feelings first and protect her little heart. It was obvious to Grace that Emma was searching for some sense of security and stability as she was making this new change in her young life. Living in Pops and Nana Gracie's home and her daddy's home, of course, was all she had ever known since her very first memory. While she loved and adored her mommy's new fiancé and was beyond excited to go on this new adventure, her little heart was feeling uneasy. Grace could feel this because she knew little Emma as well as she knew her own precious children God had given her.

Because of this, Grace knew she had a job to do. She was sure she needed to help Emma with this transition and make it as easy for her as she possibly could. It is such a natural thing when it comes to protecting God's precious little ones. For Grace, protecting Emma was second nature. After all, she had been protecting Emma since the moment God brought her into this world and blessed her family with such a sweet, tiny soul.

Grace smiled as she looked into Emma's beautiful eyes and said, "Oh, my sweet baby girl angel kisses ... you will never ever have to worry about being able to find your Pops and your Nana Gracie! We will be in this big house you have lived in for so long for a few more years at least! When we do decide we no longer need such a huge home and we decide to live in a different place, I give you my word that we will make sure you know where we live! We would want you and Joshy and all of the rest of our family to come and see us! I promise, promise, promise we would never ever move without making sure you can find us!"

Little Emma threw her arms around her Nana Gracie and told her this made her feel so much better! She also said she had a secret. Grace was a little worried about asking and decided to just let Emma navigate the conversation with her own timing. Emma smiled and said, "I did really have a tummy ache about being afraid you might move after I leave, Nana Gracie. Now, since you explained it to me and you made me your promise, my tummy doesn't hurt anymore! I also think it helped me because you were holding me and singing to me like you always do. I think I might come back and visit you so you can do it some more."

Grace realized from the words of an innocent five-year-old just how important it really is to be loving and kind. She was sure putting Emma's feelings first was the answer, as it always had been so many times before. She knew both Emma and Joshy would be leaving their precious heart prints behind in every single room of their home and in their hearts forever. She held Emma close until it was time for her to walk out the front door and into her new life. Emma never knew she took a special part of her Nana Gracie's heart that day, and Grace prayed she never would.

Chapter Eighteen

SUNDAY FUN DAY

ONCE EMMA AND JOSHY MOVED OUT ALONG WITH their sweet mommy and her fiancé, Grace found herself home alone with her broken heart. She was sincerely happy for her eldest daughter and her sweet young family, and Grace knew in her heart this was a healthy new chapter for them. Still, Grace had given so much of her heart and soul taking care of the three of them when they needed her for so long. Now, she had to find her new normal while trying to stay strong in the midst of her pain. It was always so important to Grace that she remain a strong Christian woman of faith and never burden her hard-working husband or her adult children with busy lives of their own. This wasn't always easy, but it was something she was determined to accomplish.

Grace always found comfort in doing for others. She enjoyed hosting an occasional ladies' Christian retreat or doing volunteer work. She especially loved doing for her huge family. With a family as big as the one Grace had been blessed with, there was always somewhere she was needed. Grace was more than happy to step up and make herself available for any of her family in need of her help. With Emma and Joshy no longer underfoot, Grace found herself more available for the other precious grandchildren she had been so blessed with. She and her husband absolutely loved their church and their church family and decided to invite two of their other young grandchildren to go with them one Sunday morning. Grace would never forget the smiles on their little faces when she and Pops pulled in their driveway to get them on that first Sunday morning. Both Jay and McKenna came bouncing off their front porch, smiling from ear to ear. They were so excited to attend church with their grandparents, and they couldn't wait to learn about Jesus.

This was the beginning of what became known as their family Sunday fun day! Pops and Nana Gracie would take their grandchildren Jay and McKenna to church with them every Sunday morning they possibly could. The four of them would enjoy a delicious brunch following the early morning service and talk about what they had learned in class. This was also great bonding time to simply talk about their everyday activities, friends, and school.

Before she knew it, Grace realized they had formed such a close and loving bond with both Jay and McKenna. She would not have missed this for the world. They continued their Sunday fun day for several years. Grace prayed every single time they were together that her grandchildren would never forget these precious memories they made with their grandparents. Grace knew God had heard her many prayers on the day their grandson Jay was saved and baptized to become a member of the very church they had introduced him to. This was the moment Grace realized God always puts us where we are needed most. She had always heard the saying about one door closing and another door opening. Grace never actually felt a door had closed when Emma and Joshy moved out of her home after so many years because, after all, she would always be seeing her precious grandchildren. But she now realized she had more time and room in her busy life to create the other precious bonds she so very much desired in her family. Grace was sure God had answered her many prayers on the day of her grandson's baptism. For this, she was so very grateful.

Grace was so happy that God had sent her in the direction of her other grandchildren. She was looking for her place of comfort, and this would be where God could use Grace. She knew she would never forget their many Sunday fun days together, and they were all forever closer because of them.

Chapter Nineteen

THE PHONE CALL

GRACE WAS LOOKING OUT OVER THE OCEAN THE day her Auntie June called. She wasn't exactly sure what the problem was, but she knew it was serious from the sound of her auntie's voice. Her Aunt June had always been a very strong woman in Grace's eyes, and she always seemed to be doing for others. Grace was sure this was the reason for her strength and positive attitude in life. She had always admired these qualities in her aunt and had always enjoyed hearing from her, but today felt different. She wasn't sure if they had a poor connection. Grace knew this could some-times happen because they lived right next to the ocean. Or maybe she heard something else in her Aunt June's voice. Grace listened closely as her aunt attempted to explain the reason for her phone call. Her eldest child was on his way for a liver transplant, and she knew Grace would want to know.

Grace had always been so close with her Aunt June's chil-dren, and the thoughts of any of them going through such a serious health issue absolutely took her breath away. Grace was especially close to this cousin. They were born only six weeks apart and had spent their entire childhood together. She could still remember the time in early elementary when he was in trouble for calling Grace "Sissy" rather than her birth name. This was all they had ever known, and it was a very difficult habit to change. It broke her heart to watch him struggle to remember he had to use her actual name. As Grace thought back over their childhood together, she could still remember holding his glasses on the playground so he could run and play more freely without breaking them. This memory made Grace smile as she thought about all those childhood years together.

They had always lived next door to each other, and some of her fondest memories were of when they gathered at their grandparents' home on Sunday afternoon. Their grandparents lived on a farm, which allowed plenty of room for the many grandchildren to run and be adventurous with the sun on their sweet faces and not a care in the world. Grace knew she would never forget the time that she and her cousin decided to have a competition while visiting their grandparents. Their grandfather had teased them about his tobacco and asked if they wanted to see which one of them could chew some tobacco the longest. Grace was very competitive and was determined to prove she could last longer than her cousin. She especially wanted a chance to prove girls were just as awesome as boys in every single way. Grace had no intention of allowing her cousin and a little tobacco chewing contest outdo a girl. There they stood, ready to take on their grandfather's challenge. Her cousin kept smiling and reminding her that tobacco was only for boys and would make a wimpy girl sick. Grace would just smile with her long blonde pigtails and sparkly shoes because she was sure a girl could win against a boy. She just knew he must be wrong to assume that being a boy would somehow make him superior in any area in life. Grace knew she must be representing all little girls with this challenge, and she had a job to do. She knew she had to win this contest to prove she belonged with all of the cousins playing on the farm.

Grace would never forget standing in the ditch beside her cousin, as they were both beyond ill. She could hear her elderly grandfather apologizing over and over through his laughter. She could still remember trying to convince her cousin that she had actually won and him insisting he had won while they both continued to hang their heads over the ditch. Grace had been so ill she thought it would never end. Grace knew neither of them had won that day. She also knew she never wanted to see, smell, or taste tobacco ever again. Maybe this was exactly what their grandfather had intended all along. While that was a horrible childhood experience for both of them, it would always make Grace laugh when she would think of it years later. It became one of her fondest memories of time with her cousin on the farm. Despite how awful this challenge had made them feel that day, they had once again bonded during this ordeal hanging their heads over a ditch simply sharing precious childhood days being cousins. Grace knew she loved him dearly when he had reached over and held her long blonde pigtails back while she was so ill. This was who he was to her, and she realized throughout the years they had always protected each other. Just as in most families, some cousins seem more like siblings than cousins. This was definitely the case between them. Grace always knew she could count on him, and he had meant the world to her. He was a little shy and always so very kind. Grace loved him dearly and had always been thankful for their close relationship.

"Are you there, Grace? Can you hear me?" Grace was brought back from her childhood memories as she heard her auntie softly speaking. Grace knew she had been crying. She felt she needed to help calm her. Grace started talking to her aunt, asking if there was anything she could possibly do. Speaking through her tears, she asked Grace to notify some other family members for her and, more than anything, to please pray. Grace knew the power of prayer in her life and immediately promised to do so.

Grace understood the surgery would take several hours, but she made her cousin Nicole promise she would send constant updates on her brother's surgery. Grace was so thankful for every single update she received throughout the long ordeal. Finally, after more hours than Grace could even imagine, she received news in the middle of the night that the surgeons felt they needed to close and give his body a chance to rest and heal some before continuing to repair an issue with his new liver. The thought of her cousin having surgical complications and needing further surgery broke her heart. Still, Grace knew she needed to trust God and pray. Grace continued in prayer as she waited for the next update.

Grace was so worried when she realized his surgery had started again. She knew his body had already been put through so much, and he still had such a long road ahead of him. As she prayed for her sweet cousin, her phone began to ring. He had made it through the second surgery and was headed back to the trauma ICU. While Grace knew he wasn't out of the woods yet, she was so thankful to know he still had a fighting chance.

Grace was in complete shock to find out her cousin had to have a third surgery due to complications. She knew in her heart that she needed to see him soon. Knowing the hospital was a little over two hours away, Grace began to make her travel plans. She could not wait to see him, and she realized his mother needed to see him, too. After prayerful consideration, Grace called her Auntie June and promised to take her to be with her eldest son.

Nothing could have prepared Grace for the moment she entered her cousin's hospital room in the trauma ICU. She had only known him to be a big, rather strong man. He looked so helpless and exhausted now. Grace fought back tears as she watched him hold his mother's hand. Despite his weakness and all his body had already gone through, he knew the sound of his mother's voice, and it was obvious he was pleased that she was there by his side. Grace walked to the other side of his hospital bed, trying desperately to avoid the many machines and tubes that surrounded him.

She had been here once before in her life. She could hear the sound of the machines that were helping him survive during this difficult recovery. Each noise reminded Grace of those terrifying moments spent by her own son's hospital bed in Mayo Clinic following both of his thoracic surgeries for cancer. He too had suffered complications that required multiple surgeries and a terrifying recovery. Grace remembered how important it was for her to be strong for her son and knew she needed to be just as strong for her cousin and her Aunt June. Grace softly spoke, trying to control her emotions as she asked him if he knew her. Despite all he had been through and all he obviously was still going through, he looked up at her, and as he squeezed her hand, he winked at Grace. This made Grace have to dig really deep to fight her emotions. She knew it took everything in him to try to make her feel better. Once again, she was reminded of his kind heart, and she was so thankful for their family bond.

Grace and her Aunt June had spent three days with her cousin and his lovely wife. They had been so blessed to see his other siblings and their families during their time there together. It was the end of their third day and time to return home when they realized his exhausted wife had to leave for their home for a while. As the time came for Grace and her

Aunt June to leave him, Grace knew she simply could not go home yet. She sent her Aunt June home with her daughter and made the decision to stay with her cousin. Grace was sure her aunt needed to return home for some much-needed rest, and she was just as sure she needed to stay with her cousin. Grace knew her husband would understand her decision. He was always so loving and supportive concerning their families.

Grace walked her Aunt June and her family to their car, and she could feel how comforting it was to her auntie knowing she would be staying behind to be there throughout the night for her ill son. As Grace made her way back to the trauma ICU, she prayed every step of the way. After all, Grace knew the power of prayer, and she was sure her cousin was in God's very capable hands.

Grace watched closely as the hospital staff continued checking on her cousin throughout the night. She also watched the clock because she was unable to sleep in the recliner for fear of something happening to him. As the morning sun came through the window, pouring its soft warmth over the entire room, she noticed her cousin breathing softly with the help of the machines. Grace was reminded of the early morning sun coming through her son's hospital room following his frightful ordeal in Mayo Clinic. She thought about how lasting it is to have something so beautifully ordinary as a sunrise become part of your life's journey. The sun shining down on Mayo Clinic brought forth its ray of hope for Grace and her husband as their son gradually awakened from his medically induced coma on that early October morning. As she listened to her cousin softly breathing, she realized the sun rays dancing off his ICU walls must surely be his very own rays of hope. Grace closed her eyes and began to pray once again.

Grace stayed very busy throughout the day, talking with her cousin's team of doctors and making sure she updated his wife, Auntie June, her older brother, and some other cousins as well as the rest of their worried family and friends. She tried desperately to do everything she could think of to make sure her cousin was as comfortable as possible. As the hours continued, Grace realized she couldn't leave him for the second night. Her heart was absolutely broken over all her cousin was going through. She called her husband to explain her concerns, and she was so pleased that he finished working on his own patients early so he could get on the road to be with her. Having him come to visit her cousin and offer his love and support once again reminded Grace of her many blessings in life. They shared hospital cafeteria food for dinner together so they could spend every moment by her cousin's side. Her husband's unwavering support and understanding gave Grace exactly the encouragement she needed to continue her time there in the trauma ICU with her cousin.

Once again, Grace observed the constant care given to her very ill cousin throughout the night, and once again, she watched the clock. By now she was shocked to see just how awake she continued to be despite not having gotten any sleep at all. Grace knew this must be her constant worry concerning her cousin's difficult recovery after so many complications. Just like the day before, Grace was thankful to see the sun shining through the hospital window—the same window from which Grace had watched the hospital helicopters flying back and forth from the landing pad as they continued working at all hours to save lives. She wondered if her cousin's new liver had come to him this way. Grace prayed for the organ donor who had left this world after doing one last kindness for others. She believed this had to be the most selfless act from a complete stranger. She prayed for the donor's family and asked God to somehow show them the gift their loved one had left behind. She prayed they would find comfort in knowing so many lives had been saved and given another chance because of their precious loved one. Grace knew they would never know the thoughtful and kind soul who had helped save her loved one's life. Still, she felt she needed to prayerfully thank this kind stranger and pray for the family that was going through this devastating loss.

All of this praying brought back so many memories for Grace, as she herself became an organ donor when her son was battling cancer. Seeing such endless suffering from so many families during their stay in Mayo Clinic made Grace aware of the desperate need for lifesaving organs. She recalled the moment she had witnessed firsthand the meaning of "PLEASE DON'T TAKE YOUR ORGANS TO HEAVEN. GOD KNOWS WE NEED THEM HERE," and she began to cry. As Grace wiped away her tears and attempted to relax a few minutes in the chair by the window, the head nurse came in the room and said he needed to give his patient a new medication. He was such a kind young man, and Grace had become very comfortable with him over such a long period of time together. He explained to Grace that this new medication would still keep her cousin somewhat sedated because they needed him to remain very calm during this part of his diffi-cult recovery. He also said this particular medication would make him less sleepy.

Grace was pleased to think her cousin might become more alert while she was still there. She couldn't wait for the day she could tease him about whispering in his ear over and over, "Grace is my favorite cousin. Grace is my favorite cousin." She just knew he would find this funny once he was well again. As Grace continued watching the nurse put the medication in his IV, she was so excited to think he would slowly become more and more himself.

Then it happened. As the nurse was busy gathering his supplies after administering the new medication, Grace noticed her cousin's head immediately dropped to the right, and she could no longer hear him breathing. Grace jumped to her feet, accidentally throwing her purse and everything else she was holding in her lap. She started shaking his legs and saying his name over and over. The nurse looked as if he was in complete shock. Thankfully, his reaction was short-lived, and he quickly started trying to revive his patient. As all chaos broke loose in the middle of the hospital room, another nurse came running in from the front of the ICU. Grace yelled that he had collapsed as soon as he was given the new medication. The second nurse immediately turned off the new medication as the first nurse continued giving him CPR. Grace was so grateful when her cousin started to slowly come around. Despite how truly terrifying the entire ordeal had been, Grace was just thankful God had her there looking at him during this exact moment.

Grace continued to pray for her cousin, as his recovery took a very long time in the hospital followed by rehabilitation. She was so thankful for the day he finally made his way home to work on getting his life back. Though his family and friends understood this would take a lot of determination on his part and he still had a long road ahead of him, they were all just happy he had made it this far. Grace was sure God would wrap His loving and healing arms around him as he started this next chapter. Once again, she was reminded of just how fragile life really was, and she thanked God for all of His blessings.

Chapter Twenty

THE ANTIQUE VANITY MIRROR

MANY YEARS PASSED FOLLOWING GRACE'S COUS-
in's life-threatening surgery. She had learned so much from
this experience. Most importantly, Grace learned the true
value of making herself available for family and friends in need.

Grace continued taking care of her aging parents and
being just a phone call away for her children and grandchildren. Grace kept her promise to cherish her husband
throughout their many years together as they both looked
forward to living on their South Carolina beach. They both felt
this would be the perfect place to spend the rest of their lives.

Grace could hear the waves crashing against the shore
as the ocean breeze brought the taste of the salty air into
her beautiful master suite. She and her husband had always
loved this part of beach life. They had enjoyed their lovely
beach home for so many years of their long, beautiful marriage. Their children had grown up enjoying the many sunny
hot summers gathering seashells, building sandcastles, and
swimming in the ocean. Later, their grandchildren had continued this same tradition of summertime adventures on
their favorite South Carolina beach while spending family
time together making memories. As the curtains continued

to blow softly back and forth like the wings of a graceful seagull, Grace found herself more and more relaxed. Soon, she would be resting peacefully as her mind took her away to some of the most precious days of her life. As she continued sleeping, Grace could see her children on the beach running and playing without a care in the world. Cancer had not stolen her Zachariah's innocence. Frankie had not lost his dear friends who had been taken from his life far too soon. Elizabeth had not yet experienced the tragedy of a broken heart way too young and beyond her control. Melissa, Leigh, and Brook were still tumbling across the sand in all their glory without any concern or stress for what life might have in store someday. The sun was glistening on the ocean, and she could hear their laughter so clearly as if somehow she had managed to turn back time. "Mommy! Come and help us build a sandcastle!" Grace looked up to see her children with their sun-kissed cheeks and sand-covered bodies. They were smiling with such happiness and innocence. Grace could feel their tiny childlike enthusiasm as if they had never grown up yet. Grace noticed someone in the distance, and she found herself desperately drawn to whoever this was so far away. As she looked a little closer, Grace knew it was her husband walking towards her. He was smiling as he reached for her hand. "Come take a walk with me, baby doll," he said with the sweetest smile. He and Grace had always loved walking hand in hand on the beach. They had always enjoyed searching for the most beautiful seashells to add to their collection. Grace and her husband had always cherished their time together as a couple during their long and loving marriage.

Throughout their many years together, they had strolled the romantic streets of Paris hand in hand after taking a fabulous train ride from London. They had enjoyed the sweetness of the California Napa Valley vineyards as well as the vibrant and delicious culture of New Orleans. Being president of the dental association in their home state required a great deal of traveling for her husband, and Grace was always so proud of his hard work and felt blessed to be by her husband's side in support of all of his endeavors. He always had a way of making sure she remembered how much he appreciated her and needed her with him. He had continued his education over the years and had accomplished so many dreams he had once thought impossible. But he learned with Grace by his side, he could chase his many dreams knowing she would always be there with him cheering him on with her continued prayers and encouragement.

While all of these precious memories would remain in their hearts forever, nothing compared to their time together by the ocean. As Grace continued to drift away in her sleep with the soft ocean breeze on her face, she could feel the sand between her toes as she walked on the beach with her husband. It is so strange how real something so close to one's heart can actually feel. As they continued to stroll down the beach, Grace heard her husband softly whisper, "Have I made you happy, Grace? God has blessed our marriage and our family beyond anything I could ever have imagined. I pray with everything in me I have given you the wonderful life you have given me." Just as Grace started to answer him, she felt him take her hand. It was her husband checking on her in her sleep. He wanted her to know the children and grandchildren would be there soon to visit them in their South Carolina home, and he was hoping she would feel up to it.

Grace was nearing the end of her earthly life now. She had always prayed God would call her home before He took her husband because she was sure her heart would not be able to take being on this earth without him. While the thoughts of leaving her precious children and grandchildren took her breath away, Grace knew her work here on earth was almost done. Heaven was her eternal home, and she would see them there someday. Though she was very frail and weak at this point, her husband helped Grace to her feet so she could freshen up just a little before their very short stroll on the beach as they awaited the arrival of their precious children and grandchildren.

As they made their way to her lovely antique vanity surrounded by the gorgeous South Carolina beach décor, Grace realized she now needed to lean on her husband with every step she took. As she looked into the mirror at the woman now staring back at her, Grace was so surprised by what she saw. There, in the middle of the beautiful antique vanity mirror, was the most astonishing sight. Grace could see her loved ones looking back at her. She saw her precious children—the three children God allowed to grow under her heart and the three children God had allowed to grow in her heart. Zachariah looked so strong and healthy again with his lovely family. Frankie was smiling with absolute contentment. Elizabeth was standing by her favorite soldier holding their baby. Grace could see all three of her stepdaughters surrounded by their blessings. She could see all of her precious grandchildren including future blessings she had never even met yet. She could see her parents and her siblings with their families. Both of her parents smiled as though they were thanking her for being with them during their aging years as they had been with her during her childhood.

Life really had come full circle, and Grace had always felt blessed to be there for them. Grace could see her precious grandmother and her in-laws as well as the many other relatives God had already called home. She could also see her many lovely friends she had shared her Christian walk with for so much of her life. Grace had the most beautiful memories with these same lovely ladies from their Christian retreats and life groups they had enjoyed together throughout the years. Her sweet friends Rosemary, Karena, Tessie, Claudella, Kimmie, Myla, and Gayle were smiling with such love and compassion. She looked up to see young Brent smiling as he stood there with so many blessings Grace had known during her journey in this life. She could not believe the loved ones in the beautiful antique mirror looking back at her. She turned to her husband and asked him if he could see what she was seeing. Then, as she looked back towards the mirror, she could see only herself. Then she realized she had seen all of her beautiful loved ones and their entire blessed life they had shared on this journey together in the middle of the antique mirror just as she closed her eyes for the last time. The last thing she ever saw on this earth was "the reflection of Grace" while her husband held her in his arms. Grace later opened her eyes to find herself in the arms of her Savior.

Have a kind and blessed life.

THE END

The author, Renee Eller, feeling beyond blessed with her husband Dr. David M Eller during his West Virginia Dental Association Presidency in 2017.

Renee Eller along with her husband and their six wonderful children beside the tree line behind their home in the
fall of 2017.

Photo Credit: Anora Crescent Photography

Renee Eller along with her husband, six children, daughter-in-law, and seven grandchildren praying for more precious grandchildren in their future.

Photo Credit: Anora Crescent Photography

Meet Dobby David

The Eller Family Goldendoodle

He came into their lives with his huge paws and extra huge personality full of love and cuddles. He reminded them to always love without boundaries, and they must never forget to "follow the Goldendoodle Rule."

ABOUT THE AUTHOR

RENEE ELLER LIVES WITH HER BELOVED HUSBAND, Dave, in Barboursville, West Virginia. Having raised all of their precious children, they look forward to every family gathering they can possibly share together. They both enjoy attending church together as well as their weekly Life Group, where they hear the word of God and share in fellowship.

They split their time between the gorgeous mountains of their beautiful home state of West Virginia and their ocean paradise surrounded by the shade of the swaying palm trees and the salty air on the beaches of South Carolina. They feel blessed beyond measure as a family, and they thank God for all of their many blessings every single day.

A NOTE FROM THE AUTHOR

I STARTED WRITING THIS BOOK IN THE HALLS OF Mayo Clinic during our son's battle with cancer. I found myself writing down my thoughts, my fears, my prayers, my worries, and my concerns on small pieces of paper and stashing them in my purse. Later, during the many hours of our son's aggressive chemo, I continued putting my thoughts on small scraps of paper, which eventually found their way into my notes on my cell phone. As time went on and I continued to express my feelings in my notes, I realized my writing had become a source of therapy or self-help for me as a mother. Just like a good book we all love to curl up with, my writing was something I couldn't put down. Before long, I found myself consumed with the precious memories of our lives together as I stayed by my son's side throughout his months of chemo. As I continued to allow the memories to visit my mind, they eventually made their way onto my laptop. Before I even realized what had actually happened, a book from my heart and soul was taking its rightful place in our busy lives.

I will forever be grateful to my husband and children for their love, support, and encouragement as I looked for the words I needed to express all I wanted to share. It wasn't easy to finally bring my thoughts to a close and give birth to my book. I was terrified for years that I would regret ending it too soon. I am a very thankful Christian wife, mother, and NaeNae, and I truly embrace all life has to offer. I know God has been with me every step of my journey, and I could not imagine leaving a milestone out of this precious book simply because of its timing. Then, it finally occurred to me that life will always bring us many milestones along the way, and if we are watching closely, we will be thankful for each of them until God calls us home. Not all of our precious moments will find their way into a heartfelt book of treasures to cherish, but they will forever remain in our hearts. I knew I must bring *The Reflection of Grace* to a close and thank God for His many blessings throughout our lives together.

Always stay humble and kind.

Love and prayers,

Renee Eller

CPSIA information can be obtained
at www.ICGtesting.com
Printed in the USA
FFHW011949120419
51724688-57140FF